SATURDAY'S CHILD

Marjorie Quarton

ANDRE DEUTSCH

First published 1993 by
André Deutsch Limited
105-106 Great Russell Street
London WC1B 3LJ

ISBN 0 233 988068

Phototypeset by Falcon Graphic Art Ltd
Wallington, Surrey
Printed in Great Britain by
St Edmundsbury Press, Bury St Edmunds, Suffolk

Some of the material in this book has
appeared in *The Irish Field* and
Irish Farmers' Weekly.

Contents

Illustrations between pages 90 and 91

CHAPTER ONE

STARTING YOUNG

My life, up to the age of nine or so, was so sheltered that it's a wonder I didn't suffocate. My vague early memories are of walks with my nanny, securely held by the hand, bonnetted and gaitered in the manner of the time.

I loved this nanny dearly, and wouldn't have dreamed of revealing that she pared her corns with my father's cut-throat razor. Because of those corns, our walks weren't the brisk affairs they were meant to be; most ended a few hundred yards up the road in some cosy cottage where Nanny drank stewed tea and talked to her friends about deaths and diseases.

I think that when very young I was fairly well behaved, so few scoldings and fewer slaps came my way. I was an only child so didn't have to share my parents, except with the dogs and cats which were part of the family. My mother thought I was jealous of the cat when I dropped him out of an upstairs window – and this was the only occasion when I remember her being really cross with me. In fact, I'd been told that cats always landed on their feet and was checking. (It is true.) However, my mother had seen Cromwell, so called because he was remarkably ugly, falling past the drawing room window, and I failed to convince her.

I went to so few parties that each one was an event, remembered for years. As for Christmas and birthdays, they were times for presents, but not for outings or parties. The presents were of three kinds: books, chocolates and money. The chocolates were rationed and doled out at a rate of two a day, the boxes hidden. My mother read the books to make sure they were 'suitable'; if not, they too were hidden. The money disappeared into the Post Office. I was soon an adept chocolate thief, searching the boxes out on the tops of wardrobes, and I found the books without any trouble, reading them in the airing cupboard or the cubby hole under the stairs. But the Post Office beat me: it seemed an unfair place to hide presents, as they never re-emerged. I hadn't grasped the principle of saving and wouldn't have been impressed by it if I had.

My chance to beat the system came one day when I was nine years old, just after the outbreak of the second world war. My grandmother gave me two pounds for my birthday – actually put two green pound notes into my hand. 'Get your Mummy to put it in the Post Office for you,' she said.

My mother was going to town to have her hair done, and took me with her. I was clutching my £2, so soon to disappear for ever. The hairdresser was a patient lady called Miss Ryan, who needed all her patience when I exchanged Nanny for a governess who made me learn a hymn by heart every Sunday. When my mother took me with her I sang these hymns to Miss Ryan, and my mother, deafened by the roaring

2

dryer, didn't know what was happening. As soon as she could get a word in Miss Ryan would give me twopence and tell me to run up to Gleeson's for an ice cream.

On this momentous birthday, my mother went to a different hairdresser, whose salon was in the street where sales of pigs and calves took place. I wandered out and watched. The calves were in carts, drawn up on either side of the street, with the horses facing outwards. There were also pigs, whose deafening squeals filled the air as they were prodded and pulled about.

I walked along the row of open carts looking into each one, the money crumpled in my hand. A stout man in a raincoat asked, 'Will you buy a calf, Miss?'

Buy a calf? Why not? With the Post Office waiting to swallow my money it seemed a good idea. 'How much is the roan one?' I asked. The man asked £4 (few calves were making more than £1), I craftily offered ten shillings. After spirited bargaining, in which at least a dozen bystanders joined in, I bought it for £2 and the man spat on a threepenny bit and gave it to me for luck. I then asked him to deliver the calf to my home, a distance of more than four miles. I suppose because it was so dear, he agreed fairly willingly, urged on by my supporters.

I think he was probably expecting to have to return the money and take the calf back. Instead, when he got to my home, he persuaded my father to buy the other calf, a white one, which died almost at once.

I named my calf 'Polly' after my grandmother, but this was said to be cheeky, and her full name, 'Caroline', only slightly less so. I could hardly call her 'Mrs Smithwick', and 'Granny' seemed wrong for a week-old heifer. I called her Starr in the end, after the man I bought her from. Some time afterwards, my father sold Starr for £3 and – put the money in the Post Office for me. This started in me a lifelong distrust of almost all financial institutions.

Although I became a horse dealer in my teens, when I was younger horses were the only sort of stock I never considered selling. Our carthorses worked until they died or were pensioned off or sent to the kennels. I loved them all and would have been deeply shocked if one had been sold. Cattle were another matter, and I was fascinated by the fairs which were held in the streets on the first Monday of every month. The noise, dirt and general chaos were profoundly appealing to a child kept in a nursery and bound by an unchanging routine.

The calf, pig and fowl markets, held on Thursdays, were quieter and more civilised affairs, except at Christmas. Pig dealers, who could easily be recognised by their bowler hats and the way they wore their socks outside their trouser-bottoms, were considered further down the social ladder than cattle or sheep dealers. At the Christmas markets bonhams (piglets), pork pigs and kid goats were sold, as well as every kind of poultry.

Geese were more popular than turkeys in the country, and there was a great trade for them. They used to be sold wholesale to dealers who shipped them to Liverpool, then marched them across Northern England in huge droves to Manchester, Leeds, York and even Newcastle. Geese are great walkers – fortunately – but their feet wouldn't stand up to so much roadwork. Accordingly, at the port, they were driven first through soft tar, then through sand. After this treatment, they were as good as shod. No wonder Irish geese were renowned more for muscle than for fat.

We never bought anything in the market except my calf. The turkey market was an uproarious affair, and got more so as the day progressed. Farmers' wives got few opportunities to go to the town in those days, and for many the turkeys were their only personal income. Fierce bargaining took place, and acrimonious arguments. In particular, I remember a greyhaired woman; tall, broad and determined. She wore a black hat rammed down on her head, and a man's heavy black frieze overcoat above black nailed boots. She could have shouted down any man in the market, and outsworn him too. She started a violent argument with a usually peaceable butcher about the weight of a tremendous old cock turkey. The bird, feet tied, was clutched in her powerful arms, and its face and hers were alike red and furious. Bets were laid and a crowd gathered round outside the butcher's shop. The butcher (understandably) lost his nerve and refused to weigh the bird on the spring balance in his shop. Next door was a chemist's shop, where there was a wicker basket scales for weighing babies. The lady charged into this shop and dumped the turkey in the basket, where it turned the scales at forty pounds. She then marched out in triumph to collect her winnings, without a word to the scandalised chemist.

Most riding horses, even the soberest, are terrified of pigs, yet at the market the cart-horses stood dreaming in the shafts while their passengers made a racket which could have been heard a mile away. I learned later that they had to be kept within squealing distance of a pigsty for weeks until they became accustomed to them. Even so, I can remember one of them suddenly waking up to the fact that there were a dozen little pigs in the cart behind him, and breaking into a headlong gallop. The farmer was too busy hauling on the reins to notice that the tailboard of the cart was working loose. The road was pitted with potholes and every time a wheel went into one of them, a pig fell out – about every fifty yards. The farmer, already late for the market, had first to get his horse under control, then to find somebody to hold it and lastly – the hard part – to catch the pigs.

I got one of the worst falls of my career when riding a young horse through my own front gate at a walking pace. We met my next-door neighbour's sow strolling round the corner with her family, in search of fresh grazing. The horse, named Fortune because I had thought he would make one for me, reared and fell over backwards. He landed between a tree-stump and the wall with his feet off the ground, and couldn't get up. The sow, interested, grunted and advanced a step. Fortune squealed like a mad thing and thrashed about in a panic. I wriggled out from under just as he got to his feet, broke his bridle and fled for home. I was lucky to escape with a sprained wrist, cuts and bruises. The damage to Fortune was more serious. Never again could I force or cajole him through the gate without another horse to give him a lead.

This helped me to develop a dislike of pigs almost as profound as Fortune's. Fate is said to have a sense of humour, and she demonstrated it at a garden fête in aid of some charity. I have never been able to throw straight, and when somebody persuaded me to part with sixpence to 'bowl for the pig', I didn't even try. Perhaps that was why I won the damned thing.

CHAPTER TWO

HORSE MAD

When the second world war broke out, Ireland was just recovering from a different kind of conflict – the Economic War. This was more of a deadlock than a war, but resembled most proper wars by being hardest on those who least deserved to suffer.

When de Valera, intent on a self-sufficient rural community, refused to pay annuities to England after the birth of the Free State, England imposed heavy tariffs on Irish produce. Ireland then raised her own tariffs, and the result was a crash in prices, the wholesale slaughter of calves and the ruin of farmers who depended on the cattle trade for their living.

De Valera had wanted to transfer the cattle dealers' power to tillage farmers, as tillage provided more employment than stock did. The general idea was that employment would cut down emigration, and small-holders would be able to survive, but it didn't work. Looking back over old account books, I read of bullocks bought at £14 each being sold a year later for £6. Calves were worth the price of their skins. We were lucky, having my father's pension which paid the wages and the housekeeping; others sold out to the Land Commission, becoming in effect tenants of the government. Young people emigrated in droves.

I was still a small child at the time when things were worst, but I can remember a few things about it. My father bought a small red and white heifer from an elderly widow, who had come to the house with a hard luck story. This sort of thing happened all the time: my father, who was believed (wrongly) to be wealthy, had been refusing to buy from half the countryside. The farm was already overstocked, the bank manager was getting peevish. When the woman, who was evidently desperate, explained that the heifer was all she had to keep her until harvest, my father gave her £5 for it, which was about double its market value. Even so, the woman would have had no more than ten shillings a week to live on until her acre of oats was fit to sell.

The heifer was very tame and I used later to ride on her back. We called her 'The Widow's Mite'. Unknown either to the widow or to us, the Mite was in calf, and produced a black bull calf. So we kept her for a cow and a very bad one she was.

The worst of the Economic War had passed by 1934, but farming remained bad right up to the start of the second world war, and cattle never really recovered until the seventies. I can remember the drovers who walked their cattle all day and slept at the side of the road at night, travelling from fair to fair. Some dealers could afford 'hackney cars' or taxis, but many walked their own beasts, about eight or ten miles a day in all weathers, selling as they went. In summer they put grass in their boots to keep their feet cool; on wet fair days they stood in the rain until the water ran out of their boots. Many of the drovers were ex-servicemen from the first world war, unable to survive on their pensions.

Constant wettings led to arthritis, rheumatism and consumption. On the other hand, people on the whole grumbled less, and they certainly had fewer heart attacks.

Although I spent a lot of time with farm animals, I wasn't encouraged to ride when I was small. Perhaps if a quiet pony had been provided for me, I would have been less determined to climb onto the back of any four-legged animal that would allow it.

I was brought up among the carthorses which my father had inherited along with the farm. They were big, heavy animals with soup-plate feet, sad white-blazed faces and gentle natures. I was happy enough clumping around on their broad backs until I saw the foxhounds in full cry. Then I began to dream of speed and thrills and to beg for a pony. For what seemed to me like many years, I begged in vain.

Recently, I was sorting through a box of old photographs when I found one of myself on one of my first horses: Fred, a bay gelding of Clydesdale type about 16.2 hands high (for those unfamiliar with horses, the 'hand', by which they are measured at the shoulder, equals four inches, so Fred was five foot six). I am wearing a tidy jacket and a pair of pint-size jodhpurs, made by Mr Condon the tailor. (I remember sitting on his counter, drawing faces on somebody's cut-out suit in tailor's chalk.) My feet are in the stirrup leathers, because my legs are too short to reach the irons. I am profoundly happy. I recall my mother shouting from a window, 'A hat! The child must wear a hat!' She, of course, was picturing me being dragged by one of those stiff, curling stirrup leathers and probably killed; she meant a hard hat. I slid off Fred (it was like sliding down a roof), ran indoors and clapped a hat on my head. To me at five years old, a hat was a hat. The one I am wearing in the snapshot is a broad-brimmed affair in yellow straw with a wreath of buttercups and satin bows.

When Fred died I tried riding Packy, a black horse with a nasty temper from having been backed under heavy loads who used to turn his head and snap at my toes with long discoloured teeth. I begged and begged for a pony. At last, when I was about seven, I got Martin. He was only 13.2 hands, but he was a cob rather than a pony: a thickset roan with a mind of his own. The idea was that he would be useful on the farm when I had outgrown my passion for riding. He certainly did his best to cure me, usually by stopping dead and dropping his head. I would slide bumpily, head first, down his bristly hogged mane, and Martin would tip me over his ears and trot away. Since this happened every time I rode him – sometimes several times during one ride – I decided to try something safer, namely either the Widow's Mite or a red cow called Adelaide. I rode them in from the field at milking time, and both were far better schooled than Martin – not that that was saying much.

I suppose I had a way with animals, because I had little trouble in taming and training the cattle. I never tried saddling one, but as soon as I was tall enough to get onto their backs I took to riding the bullocks round the fields. I made string halters for them and gave them names. One of my favourites was called Blue Peter after the Derby winner of that year.

At last my parents decided that such dedication deserved a better mount, and horrible Martin was exchanged for Pippin. She had a hollow back, which made a nice change: cattle are not designed by nature for bareback riding.

I now became a standard horse-mad child, convinced that all time not spent with ponies or horses was wasted. I remember, but can't place, a verse I read years ago, which must have described the feelings of many parents, certainly my own:

I love my child – I like the horse –

10

But this is what is sad:
The two together, night and day,
Will drive me mad. . . .

Always a voracious reader, I turned from Sir Walter Scott's
Waverley novels, through which I had been doggedly worrying my way, and read only 'pony books', a genre which must
have had its day – I don't see many of them in the shops now.
Probably girls of from ten to fourteen years old mostly read
adult books, comics or teenage romances. In the 'forties, pony
books were everywhere and I had a cupboard full of them in my
room. They had titles such as *A Pony for Penelope*, *A Hunter for
Henrietta*, *A Cob for Kate*. They were never called *A Gelding
for Gideon* or *A Filly for Philip* because they weren't written for
boys. The children were always female, about twelve years old
and spoiled rotten. The ponies on the other hand were usually
male, about 13.2 and only partly spoiled, so that Penelope or
Kate could sort them out in time to win the bending race in
the last chapter. (These books were always illustrated, often
beautifully, so the not so well informed could see just what a
bending race was. To the non-horsey it suggests a gymnastic
competition.)

I used to think that some day I would write a pony book
of my own (*A Mare for Marjorie*), and I made several attempts
to start one. The problem was that the books were written to
a formula outside my experience. They were generally set in
the Home Counties of England, where kind Mummies and
Daddies bought ponies for their children as a matter of course.
The Daddies, although generous, were uninterested. They spent
their working hours in London offices and their leisure playing
golf. The Mummies, once horsey little girls themselves, were
more helpful.

Although the story lines were simple, the language was
not. 'Isn't he a teeny bit overbent, darling?' Mummy would
enquire anxiously (all those bending races). Or 'Do be careful,
Samantha, Topper's getting behind his bit.'

11

I wondered where else could a pony be in relation to his bit except behind it? Ahead of it? Surely not.

The books were always full of instruction about riding and stable management, sometimes sound, sometimes not. I learned a good deal. Some of the terms defeated me and it was no good asking my father who despised the books heartily. I asked a friend to translate Samantha's request, 'Mummy, shall I give Topper a direct aid?' and Mummy's solemn reply, 'Very well, darling. Just this once.'

'A direct aid's a crack down the ribs with an ashplant,' said my foxhunting friend.

I filed this information away, wondering why Samantha couldn't be more explicit.

How I envied those spoilt little girls with their yellow polo-necked jerseys, their velvet caps, jodhpurs and shining jodhpur boots. My own jodhpurs had been outgrown within weeks. I was growing like a willow and my riding dress consisted of boys' corduroy shorts, snake-buckle belt, bare legs and sandshoes. The top half of me was dressed in anything that came handy. My saddle was kept for special occasions, partly because it was unlikely to be replaced, partly because the leathers pinched my bare knees and the irons chafed my bare insteps. I rode much better without a saddle, anyway.

As I grew older, I realised that I was luckier than Kate, Samantha and the rest of them, because they had to clean all their tack every day and were hedged around with rules and regulations. ('Darling! You can't go riding like that! You've not oiled Pixie's hooves.') When my girth burst out hunting, I hung the saddle on a gate and continued happily without it until nightfall. When I got home, I couldn't remember which gate I'd left it on and there was trouble, so I got my bike and found it at last. Samantha would have had her pocket money stopped for that.

Of course by the time I was ten or eleven years old, my life had ceased to be sheltered. Europe was at war, the last of my governesses had gone and I was left to my own devices. My parents seldom made a fuss as long as I appeared at mealtimes – but there was one time when I was in real trouble. I was obliged to wear a plate to straighten my teeth and it flew out of my mouth as I fell off into a deep ditch. I didn't see any reason to search for the hated object, but my parents did and I had to go back to the place every day and look for it. The search was abandoned after a week and my teeth stayed crooked.

The children in the pony books were easily pleased when it came to presents. Acceptable gifts included stable rubbers, neckstraps, curry-combs and curbchains. I distinctly remember a child being thrilled when Mummy presented her with a bucket and broom for mucking out.

The information in the pony books stopped short at breaking in. For this, I turned to Western movies, so I believed it was done by lassooing a horse and allowing it to buck itself to a standstill. The rider would then bound on to its back, waving a ten-gallon hat and shouting, 'giddy-ap' or some such encouragement, whereupon the horse was said to be broken in. It could be bridled and, with a maximum of rearing and frothing at the mouth, controlled. Nothing could have been further from the schooling received by my pony heroes.

The first animal I tried to break in myself was a two-year-old pony filly which was being grazed on the farm for the summer. I was eleven years old and made up in recklessness what I lacked in sense. I lowered myself onto her back from the branch of a tree, having haltered but not bitted her. I think she was too astonished to buck, or perhaps she didn't know the rules for broncos.

I had been riding her for a week before I tried putting a bit in her mouth, and the only time she ever bucked was the first time she was saddled. My parents had no idea what I was up to until then. After that, my father explained about mouthing, long-reining and backing, and I broke in another pony.

Most of my tack was made up of odds and ends of trap harness. For reins, I used lampwick, a lovely soft substance which I haven't seen for years, ideal for the job. The rotten leather constantly broke, and was replaced with lengths of doubled twine or with wire. I was also adept at riveting the broken ends together.

In my late teens, I moved on to training horses both to saddle and harness for pay – if you could call it that. The going rate was £5 for about a month's work, and included necessary expenses such as shoeing. When I upped my price to £7, my customers complained bitterly.

Mostly, the horses were neither well-fed nor well-bred enough to give me much trouble, but I earned my money with the others. One of them, a ewe-necked grey, had his head set on at such a curious angle that it was impossible to mouth him properly. I clamped his head down with a standing martingale and took him out hunting. After a spectacular succession of rears and fly-jumps, he broke the martingale and ran away with me down a nearly vertical slope, dotted with gorse bushes. The slope lay between the Killaloe road and the Castlelough graveyard. As my mount hurtled downwards, I felt we were heading for the right destination.

We rolled the last dozen yards and I escaped with nothing more serious than a earful of mud – literally. I had to go to the doctor to have the last of it removed.

Soon afterwards, this horse's owner took him to Limerick Fair and sold him as 'regularly hunted by a lady'. I didn't hear of this description until after he had been sold to Tommy Grantham, who asked me if I was the lady in question. He also asked if I had got the grey ready for the fair. I then learnt that his mane had been plaited in long pigtails, each finished off with a bow of blue hair-ribbon.

Samantha's Mummy would have been horrified.

CHAPTER THREE

SATURDAY'S CHILD

The nanny mentioned earlier, who looked after me when I was small, naturally had days off. My mother then took charge of me, rather nervously. She was not of the generation which bathes and changes its babies, and my father was eighteen years older. Later, as an only child, I was much in the care of housemaid, cook or even ploughman, and each competed to spoil me. The only time when the spoiling flagged was when I didn't want to go to bed, and the poor girls who were supposed to look after me wanted to go out and meet their boyfriends. Because of this, I was taught that once in bed it was wise to stay there for fear of bogy men. As well, I learned always to keep my hands under the sheets; this was to discourage thumb-sucking I believe. I was told that the child who was foolhardy enough to leave so much as a finger out of bed might have it taken and shaken by an ice cold hand, while a menacing voice asked, 'How are you keeping this fine night, Miss Marjorie?' It was many years before I outgrew my fear of the phantom hand.

As soon as I was old enough, I began to help with the calves and around the yard, and was encouraged to do this. I was not encouraged to help indoors; when I married in my mid-thirties my housekeeping was a joke and I had no idea how to cook for a family. Years of being shooed out of the kitchen had made me even more undomesticated than my mother, if that was possible.

Outside, I got underfoot quite a lot and helped a little. I learned to milk, to separate the cream, to churn and make butter. I learned to teach calves to drink from a bucket by letting them suck my fingers in the milk then taking the fingers away. I learned that calves had a habit of dying.

Looking back, I think we must have lost about one calf in four. Of course there were no antibiotics and the value of calves was small, but we tried valiantly to keep them alive. They were sewn into sacking jackets if they got pneumonia, and dosed with frightening mixtures. A 'green bottle' containing arsenic among other things, was a tonic; a 'black bottle' (treacle, liquorice, linseed oil) was a sovereign remedy for pneumonia; a 'brown bottle' contained ginger, honey and poteen. This was a kill-or-cure medicine which cured seldom. Poteen on its own could almost raise the dead if not overdone – it is still sold as a medicine.

As I got bigger, I progressed to driving the carthorses. Paddy, the ploughman, was endlessly patient, so was Edmund, the herd. At Paddy's house, as a small child, I sat on his knee eating oranges and drinking goat's milk, or listened while he played the Harvest Time Jig on his melodeon. The time would come when these men would have to take orders from me, and I would have to try to keep their respect without losing their affection. I was lucky in managing to achieve this, and both stayed on until they retired.

16

By the time I was twelve I could drive most horse-drawn implements. My father wouldn't have a tractor on the place, so until he died, many years later, I worked horses in shafts and in chains, single and double. The heavy horses had been replaced by clean-limbed, active Irish Draughts – an unwelcome change for the workmen who had grown used to a leisurely pace. I never tried ploughing because Paddy, very sensibly, wouldn't let me, and I only once drove three horses in the reaper and binder, but I tried everything else.

Driving the swath-turner in the hayfield was one of the most boring jobs on the farm, and one often allocated to me. I wanted to drive the tumbling rake, a flat affair which gathered the hay into piles. When the rake was full the driver would lift a wooden handle which made the rake somersault and deposit its load of hay for 'tramming', as it was called in my area. The word 'tram' for a haycock was a shortening of 'tramp-cock', which came from the trampling-down of large cocks as they were built, to make them firm. The tumbling rake was not an implement to daydream behind. If it was carelessly tumbled the tines could stick in the ground and impale the driver; if the horse stopped suddenly, the rake could turn over against his back end. I wasn't allowed to drive the tumbling rake until I was twelve.

Windrowing hay with the wheelrake was heavy work for a child, but it was one of my regular jobs for years. My favourite workhorse was a grey of uncertain temperament called Paul. He was a light draught, sired by the great local horse Jack Steel. Paul walked so fast in chains that I almost had to run to keep up with him. This was probably why there was so little competition to drive him. In the wheelrake, he strode along, his handsome head in the air, his ears pricked. It was like driving a good hunter.

Ecologists bewail the scarcity of corncrakes, skylarks, butterflies and various other birds and insects. So do I. But I do not regret the passing of the wild black bee. I expect some of them are still around – it is usually gentle creatures that become extinct – but they no longer nest on the ground in hayfields. As long as I live, I will never forget the day Paul put his hoof in a bees' nest.

I was turning the rake at the end of a swath and, as I was only just tall enough to press the lever which lifted the teeth of the rake, I was standing on it. This was mildly dangerous, like standing on the pedals of a too high bicycle, but necessary, as I needed both hands for the reins. Paul suddenly leaped forward, I fell back, grabbed the seat and just missed falling under the rake. At the same moment, two bees stung me, on the face and neck.

The seat of an old-fashioned wheelrake is high, hard and precarious. Its wheels are high too, and fastened to the axle with a single pin for easy removal. I clung to the seat with one hand, the reins with the other, my foot still on the lever. Bees whizzed past my ears as Paul raced across the field as fast as he could lay leg to the ground. Paddy and Edmund, who had been 'heading' the trams made the day before, began to run, shouting advice. Then, I think, they began to pray.

Paul kept going until a wheel came off the rake; then he swung round in a circle, and stopped as I tumbled on to the ground between his heels and the tines of the rake. Heaven knows why he stopped – if he hadn't, I wouldn't be writing this. I crawled out, my face swelling from the stings. I have been terrified of bees ever since.

A neighbour of mine, Jack Quinlan, had a similar accident with a wheelrake some years later, but his horse – a three-year-old – didn't stop and he was seriously hurt. I bought that three-year-old for £38 and she later became an international showjumper, changing hands for the then unheard of sum of £9,000. Her name was Sugar Bush.

When I started breaking horses to harness, as soon as they were mouthed I would attach them to a 'clod-crusher'. This implement was a primitive device if ever there was one, being merely a slab of slate drawn by two chains. The idea was that there was little of value for the youngster to break, but it was slow work walking behind on the ploughed and harrowed ground. One could, of course, if suicidally inclined, ride on the clod-crusher, as on a skateboard, and I sometimes did this.

When I think of those great rough creatures with their iron mouths and huge feet, and remember the crazy things I did with them, I realise that I must have led a charmed life. The only major disaster I can recall took place in harvest time, when there was a rush on and, as well as a young horse, the gardener and the postman had been pressed into service. It was wartime, and we were obliged to till more land than we had horses or hands to work.

I was driving the young horse, a blocky little short-striding animal called Stumpy. I was riding on the first of two loads of wheat coming up the narrow, stony lane from the field to the farmyard. Stumpy slipped and fell, both shafts snapped and the entire load of corn landed on top of the horse with myself somewhere in the middle of it.

Paul, drawing the second cart, had no room to get by, and as he became frightened, the postman daren't leave his head. I couldn't move either, having been almost knocked out by a violent blow under the chin from the hames: we waited for someone to find us.

Someone came eventually, the load was forked off and Stumpy got up, his knees streaming with blood. I got into big trouble over that. But when I look at the place where it happened over forty years ago, I wonder how horses ever pulled loads over those slippery rocks without falling. They must have led charmed lives too.

My favourite task when I was about ten was driving the pony and trap – provided I was allowed to do so alone. Somebody had told me that if I drove the pony fast enough, he wouldn't have time to fall. There is a serious flaw in this reasoning, but he never did. On Sundays, I decanted my parents at the Church door and then drove the pony to Jerry's Yard, the livery stable, as fast as he could go. We tore straight down the main street and took the right-angled turn on one wheel. Having handed the pony over to Jimmy Reardon or his father Jack (I don't remember a Jerry), I ran all the way back, taking a short cut through the Catholic church grounds and arriving at the Protestant establishment when the service was well under way.

At last the Rector's wife suggested that I should sit in the gallery at the back as I disturbed the worshippers when I charged panting up the aisle. That is how I joined the choir – musical ability had nothing to do with it.

In the war years, many people drove really fast horses, and road races were popular. One in particular, the subject of astonishing wagers, took place after a funeral. The distance was seven miles, from Toomevara to Nenagh, and a grey thoroughbred mare was made favourite. In the end she was beaten by a half-hackney. This horse, a black, used to trot with his head right up in the air and twisted to one side, while gobbets of froth from his mouth blew back and splattered his driver all over.

Hackneys were not generally admired in Ireland. 'Lifting up his feet like a turkey in a stubble field,' said one scornful observer. However, the black was unbeatable at trotting.

Horse racing on the Dublin road today is unimaginable – even hacking on the roads can be fairly hazardous. No wonder that modern children sometimes look more as if they were about to play American football than to go for a quiet ride along the road. Cars travel faster, tractors are much larger than they once were and alarmingly gaudy plastic is everywhere. Plastic bags are draped over every hedge after a spring gale, lorries with huge flapping covers tear along country lanes, and rally drivers practise controlled skids on hairpin bends. It occurs to me that each generation of horses is born with less fear than the one before. Just as our forbears would have had hysterics if they had found themselves in a jet plane, so the horses at the beginning of our century almost fainted at the sight of a motor car. The car might be a little box-like thing, chugging along at fifteen miles an hour, but it could cause as much terror as a fire-breathing dragon.

Present-day horses are as blasé about traffic as present-day children are about air travel. Oddly enough, this is the case even when the horse has been bred in some remote spot, seeing no traffic at all. Do they learn from their mothers that there is nothing to fear? I feel it may have something to do with the people who handle them. Expecting that a horse will shy is the surest way to make him do so. I once took a horse for schooling, having been told nothing except that he was as green as a cabbage, and rode him for miles without mishap, wondering why he'd been sent to me. There wasn't much traffic, but what there was he ignored. Finally, I rode him right through the town. No problem. Baffled, I asked his owner about him. She said he had shied her off more than once. A nervous rider, she used to dismount as soon as a car came in sight, and hold his head until it had gone.

The next time I rode this horse, he was quite bad in traffic. He spooked and sidled and tried to turn round. I am sure this was because I now knew his history and was sending him messages of anxiety through the reins. This horse was sold soon after, and gave no trouble to his new owners, safe in their blissful ignorance.

In the hills near my home, the winding roads have for many years been popular with those who fancied their chances as rally drivers. One such was a young Englishman who, about forty years back, decided to try out his new sports car on a mountain called Pallasmore. The car was a low slung MG with a long bonnet with a strap round it. As the young man roared round a bend, he overtook an old man driving a binder; two horses on the pole, a third tied to the back. The effect of the MG's appearance was electric

21

– the driver managed to pull it up, but the binder was away.

The three horses bolted almost a mile down a steep and winding hill. At the bottom was Carrickmadden Bridge, hardly wider than the binder and set at a slight angle. The old man, a fine horseman in his day, had been hanging on to the reins grimly, concentrating on steering his team. Never for a moment losing his head, he steered his horses safely across the bridge: the hard pull up the valley on the opposite side stopped them most effectively.

'I'm so terribly sorry,' said the young man.

What the old man said is not on record.

CHAPTER FOUR

UNWILLING TO SCHOOL

T he outbreak of the second world war is constantly being
recalled in books by people who were children at the time.
Many claim to have known at once that 'nothing would ever be
the same again', and to have been deeply worried about the out-
come. I remember the radio announcement – or at least I think
I do. The general feeling in our household was that Hitler was
a Bad Man, therefore Germany couldn't possibly win. I doubt
if this was how my parents really felt, but it was certainly the
comforting impression they gave to me.

My father, like most of those who fought their way right
through the 1914–1918 war, was reluctant to talk about it. I
begged for gory stories in vain. He claimed that if a man stated
that he had waded through blood, he generally turned out to

23

have spent the war in Cornwall or Aberdeen. As a result, I wasn't surprised when he was unwilling to talk to me about this new war. He and my mother became preoccupied and silent. I found I was free of discipline, and could run wild all day unpunished. There were many times when I doubt if I was missed.

My parents began to spend their time listening to news bulletins on the wireless (whose batteries constantly had to be recharged, and were often flat when most needed). My father studied maps; my mother developed asthma. It was years before I understood that it was brought on by worry about her sisters, living between London and the coast.

If my parents discussed the situation – as they must have done – they didn't do so when I was around. By the time I was old enough to take the war seriously, it was almost won.

In Ireland in 1939, we had plenty of meat and dairy produce, but oil, tea and other imported goods disappeared almost overnight. There was of course a black market, but even this soon ran short of petrol coupons. As for clothing, it must have been a headache for the mother of a huge child like me, who was growing all the time. I remember her making me a dress out of my bedroom curtains, and a number of hand-me-downs donated by adults of various shapes and sizes, cut in the styles of a decade earlier.

There were few tractors, and our stately Morris Cowley was one of the very few cars in this out-of-the-way area; even so, the absence of any kind of oil had a dramatic effect on everyday life.

We had plenty of horses, but our traps and harness were ancient and rotten. At first, there was a small ration of petrol; soon it stopped. During the 1940 invasion scare, all farmers were ordered to place obstacles in their larger fields to prevent planes from landing; what kind of obstacle wasn't specified. A neighbour, not wishing to impede his ploughing, erected a row of tall poles along the edge of a quarry. Our vehicles – a gig, a sidecar and a brougham – looked odd and neglected scattered about in our largest field. I doubt if they would have delayed an invasion for long.

At that time, I was doing lessons with a girl of my own age, at my home. We were taught by a young woman who drove an Austin Seven. When the petrol went, so did she. I was almost ten at the time, and it was the end of any regular education for the duration of the war. My parents took it in turn to teach me for an hour or so at a time, and I was happy with the arrangement.

Most people prefer to teach subjects they are good at and my parents were no exception. They were both fond of poetry and well versed in literature, so I got double helpings of that subject. My mother taught me literature, Scripture, botany, French and geography; my father taught me literature, Latin, Euclid, astronomy and ancient history. Nobody taught me arithmetic or modern history, but it was my parents, not the teachers who came later, who made me appreciate the English language.

When I was fourteen and a half, my education was gradually abandoned and I assumed that I was now an adult. There had been a plan to send me to boarding school in England – I used to have nightmares about it. Then, on VE day, in the middle of the school year, I was sent off to school in Dublin.

This is supposed to be a happy book, but it is also my own story. Adults who ought to know better have a nasty habit of saying 'Your schooldays are the happiest of your life,' which may be true for some. Not for me. I was intensely miserable for the two and a half years that followed. Trained in the stiff upper lip school, I had learned never to complain; which, as it happened, was almost the end of me later on, when I failed to complain of a severe pain. A burst appendix was removed just in time.

It didn't occur to me to argue when the school brochure

arrived, and I didn't even consider simply refusing to go. Now, I feel sure that my parents would have taken me back home if they'd had any inkling of my misery, but they didn't know. I had received what seemed to me like a long prison sentence, undeserved and grossly unfair, but I endured it without a word of protest.

The school in question was then six miles from Dublin – now the area is built up. Possibly it was a good school. It was located in an enormous and viciously cold Palladian house of great historic interest. Our classrooms had Adam mantelpieces, floor-to-ceiling mirrors and double mahogany doors with cut crystal handles. When I heard last year that the house had been pulled down, I felt a pang of regret; when I was there, I would gladly have helped to demolish it.

My problem was that I had been brought up in almost total isolation from my own age group. I was four years old when I first saw a baby, and my ideas about them were founded on the koochi-koo type of pictures on the tins which held Allen and Hanbury's rusks. Nanny took me to see our neighbour's new son who was lying on his back on a rug; eyes screwed shut, fists in the air. He was bright pink and motionless. My innocent question, 'What is it? Is it cooked?' earned me a stinging slap and a scolding. My yells woke the baby who added his own, and I realised my hideous mistake. I was not easily forgiven.

At school I did a test which showed me to have progressed as far as simple division. I was placed in form IV B with ten-year-olds, and also in a dormitory where I was the eldest by far. I suffered from a form of mainly non-violent bullying, but my reading (*Tom Brown's Schooldays*, *Eric: or Little by Little*,) had prepared me. YOU MUST NOT TELL. I didn't tell. In her wonderful novel *Cat's Eye*, Margaret Atwood describes the technique of my persecutors so exactly that I could hardly bear to read it, even now.

The school was tiny. In my first year there were only about thirty boarders, aged from six to seventeen. The teaching was good – with a teacher/pupil ratio of around eight to one that could be expected. I found my level by degrees. I passed my exams in due course, but my only scholastic record was an incredible eight per cent in a maths exam – a record which, I believe, remained unequalled. After that, piano practice was replaced by extra maths, but I never learned. This is odd, as I can do problems in my head quickly. If you are going to buy a bunch of cattle and you know they weigh 325.75 kilos and that a fair price would be £107.50 per hundred kilos, you have to think fast in an auction ring. Using a calculator brands you as a wimp, or – worse – an agricultural adviser.

To say I was homesick at school is an understatement. I yearned for my home, family and animals. There were no home weekends or half-term holidays for me; petrol was still a problem and trains were slow and unpredictable. The other girls seemed to me – solitary and eccentric as I was – to be as alien as Martians. Naturally they disliked me. I made only one real friend, and she left to complete her education in England.

Some of the girls went for weekly riding lessons with the late Colonel Joe Hume Dudgeon, an international horseman of great repute. I didn't go because my father taught me at home. He was an excellent horseman and a high-handicap polo player in his day. Unlike many army men of his generation he was practical rather than hidebound. For example, he didn't teach me to mount facing the horse's tail. He held that with a green horse, and most of mine were green, you should keep your eye on the front end and to hell with the book. I appreciated my father's teaching, but it didn't stop me from being green with envy as I watched the others going off for their riding lessons.

The Dudgeon horses were far removed from riding-school hacks, except for the wooden-quiet ponies provided for beginners. One of the horses was a winner of the Irish St Leger called Ochiltree. At that time a racehorse, if a gelding, had little value once he stopped winning. We used to see Reynoldstown, a dual winner of the Grand National, drawing a dog-cart in Dundrum.

The winter of 1948 was the worst since records began. In Ireland, we weren't used to hard weather, or prepared for heavy snow, so there was chaos in the cities, and country places were cut off without supplies. Most of the pupils were sent home, but I was one of half a dozen with measles. We and a skeleton staff stayed on. As we recovered, and could have gone home, the blizzards returned and we were cut off from supplies of milk, coal and bread. The only plentiful food was cornflakes, flour and dried apricots. The power lines collapsed and left us in the dark. We had to stay in bed in order to keep warm. It was a week until the avenue was cleared.

At that time petrol was slowly returning and horses were two a penny. This combined with hungry war-torn Europe to encourage the shipping of live horses for slaughter. During the cold spell of 1948, a lorryload of horses destined for the continent got stranded near my school. Presumably the driver, unable to get any further, let down the ramp and turned his cargo loose to scavenge. Poor things, they wandered about among the new suburban bungalows, looking for food. Some were caught and taken to the pound, but four remained hanging round the school all winter. One of them, a nice grey mare with a bit of breeding, used to come to the kitchen door for scraps: a gentle creature, only three years old. We used to save bread and potatoes for her. One day she disappeared and we didn't see her again.

The high spot of the summer for me occurred when another girl and I were allowed into Dublin for the day with the housekeeper. This housekeeper was an attractive girl, only a few years older than we were, and equally impatient of authority. Instead of shopping – difficult on ten shillings (50p) a *term* – we went to Phoenix Park races.

I was ferociously bitten by a flea on the bus, and it seemed as good a reason as any to put two weeks' pocket money on a two-year-old, hideously named 'The Bug'. The horse duly obliged at seven to one, and I spent the rest of the day losing my winnings piecemeal, and scratching.

Back at school, we used to bet on the Grand National, giving our pennies and sixpences to Cooney, the odd-job man who put them on for us. The first post-war race was won by Lovely Cottage, and a girl who lived in one backed him. Most of us went for the great Prince Regent who, having been in training when the race was in abeyance, must have been one of the best horses *not* to win a National. Prince Regent was clobbered with weight that year and the next, still being placed both times. The second time we had learned caution and hedged our bets.

One girl put a shilling on Caughoo because she had a cold and his name sounded like a sneeze. Cooney backed a better fancied horse for her, because Caughoo was at 100/1 and he didn't like to throw a schoolgirl's money away. But Caughoo won.

The school was one of those which do not encourage the competitive spirit. I never quite understood the principle of this, but I think it's akin to being virtuous for virtue's sake, not because of a fear of hell fire. One was expected to do one's best without marks, good or bad. 'Remarks' used instead, ran in descending order from excellent to unsatisfactory. Games, however, couldn't be organised along these lines, and we were terrors on the hockey field and the netball pitch. After matches with other schools, we would travel back on the bus, proudly displaying our wounds. Black eyes and hacked shins were all in the day's work. We were considered very tough for Protestants. Hockey is a rough game, but roughest when played by Convent girls, whose games mistresses were nuns. I particularly remember the fighting tactics of the girls of St Mary's, Haddington Road.

I think the competitive spirit is built in rather than acquired – something primitive to do with survival I daresay. I know that it is addictive. A love of racing is part of this fondness for competition: it too is addictive, and I'm not talking about compulsive gambling. From childhood games like tag and hide-and-seek, the racing addict proceeds by way of bicycles to greyhounds, fast cars or horses. I, along with some of my companions at school, became addicted to snail racing.

The craze started when we all backed Prince Regent to win at Leopardstown. We hadn't much knowledge of betting, except that if the horse won so would we. The Prince won at long odds on and our sixpences were turned to sevenpences. Disillusioned, we decided on a new sport, betting to be limited, and organised by ourselves.

We collected our snails at the bottom of the garden, and transferred them to their training quarters in the domestic science kitchen. There, we raced them along teatrays towards a dish of lettuce. As they tended to stop and fraternise, we erected rulers and raced them along tracks.

We painted their shells in our racing colours. Mine wore light blue and claret hoops on his – or possibly her – shell. The fastest snail, a very large specimen called Semolina, was owned and trained by a girl called Maeve Dring. She – Semolina that is – was bright blue with black spots, and her track record was twenty-four inches in twelve minutes, or two inches a minute.

After a while, the headmistress discovered what we were up to in the domestic science kitchen. Was she relieved? No. The snails were banished, and we were told off for cruelty to animals. In vain we pleaded that the snails loved racing and that the training was all done by kindness. We were ordered to release them in the wild, or more precisely at the bottom of the tennis court.

Now comes the part you won't believe, but I'm not joking, it's true. About a fortnight later, at prayers, one of us was pounding out a hymn on the grand piano and the rest of us were singing. Suddenly I noticed a large, bright blue snail with black spots clinging to the leg of the piano. Semolina had come home.

A day or so later I found my own snail, named Troubadour Romance after a fast two year old of his year, climbing up the wall of the house towards the same window that Semolina must have used. By degrees, five of the stable of eleven came home. They had travelled, hedge and dyke so to speak, all of a hundred and fifty yards.

A word of warning to anyone who might want to try the riveting sport of snail racing. You mustn't paint their shells with anything heavier than watercolours or they will die. Enamel looks great but it's lethal.

Those of us who are afflicted by the racing bug will match anything that has legs or wheels or, in extreme cases, creatures which have neither.

Towards the end of my time at school I had to make up my mind whether I wanted to go to University and try for a degree in modern languages, or whether I wanted to go home and be a working farmer. But I hadn't any choice, really: my father was unwell and without anyone to succeed him there, he would have sold the place. Already I was buying and selling cattle for him in my school holidays. I went home.

CHAPTER FIVE

GOING TO THE DOGS

Life down on the farm was pretty boring for me when I left school. I'd imagined I would have some say in the running of the farm, but my father's health had improved in a big way, so I was still no more than spare cheap labour. I thought of ways to save time and work, but they found no favour. My work was mostly with the livestock; partly because I liked animals better than machinery, partly because I could run. My God, how I ran! It was some time before it occurred to me, sprinting after some wayward heifers, that I wasn't even the under cow-girl or assistant carter. I was the dog.

At that time, there were no sheep on the farm. There were, on the other hand, any number of cows, calves, bullocks and

33

heifers, all of them convinced that the grass was greener on the other side of the fence. There is also the curious fact, seldom mentioned by zoologists, that all cattle, male and female, castrated or not, firmly believe that they are bulls. This can make herding difficult. Edmund had a succession of cattle dogs, but most were of the sort that is better at barking than anything else except perhaps eating and sleeping. They also usually chose the wrong place to bark – such as standing in the gate I was trying to drive the cattle through. This was guaranteed to fray an already uncertain temper. I asked if I might have a dog of my own.

When we'd been snowed up at school, the blizzards had continued well into March in the Dublin mountains. It was there that I'd first seen a sheepdog at work. The scene was by no means typical. The dog had just discovered the place where about twenty sheep had been buried alive in the snow for more than a fortnight. Led by the dog, a group of men had found the chamber, much like an igloo, where the surviving sheep were huddled. It was like a tiny, evil-smelling room with brown glass walls. The heat which gushed out was extraordinary – almost as powerful as the stench.

The dog had moved away, nose down, and was scratching at a slight hump on the ground; but there was nothing under the snow but a sad heap of frozen wool. A farmer, resting on his spade, remarked, 'Ah, a good dog is worth seven men.' At the time this seemed like a feeble joke to us, but he was right.

Denied a herding dog of my own, I did my best to train my mongrel terrier Sam for the work. Sam wasn't short of brains, but there was no collie in his mixed ancestry, and he hadn't the built-in authority which forces cattle and sheep to obey a herding dog. Sam just got chased and kicked, so I returned to my running and swearing.

When Sam died, I was without a dog for a while. I'd started dealing in horses and was being kept busy enough not to be bored, so I didn't mind too much.

34

Nowadays, I'm often assured that I must be a 'great dog-lover'. What, I wonder, *is* a doglover? It must be impossible to love the whole canine race, chihuahua and bull-mastiff alike. I like dogs – deserving dogs, that is – and a few have meant more to me than most humans, but I don't care to be labelled 'doglover' . . . or to be labelled at all, for that matter.

That said, I must admit that even the most cynical can be won over by a litter of cuddly puppies. Strong men drool and go '. . . A-a-a-aaah . . .' This is sentiment. I have learned to be more impressed by a responsible attitude towards adult dogs, having seen too many spoilt puppies grow into spoilt dogs. They rule their owners, and sometimes terrorise postmen while welcoming burglars.

Nothing could be more spoilable than a six-week-old beagle puppy, or his larger relative, the foxhound: soft floppy ears, silky skin, appealing expressions . . . I could go on. I have reared dozens and the two that stick in my mind were called Tearful and Terrible.

Young foxhounds, like young guide dogs, are 'put out to walk' for much of their first year. They go to farm homes where they get good food, individual attention and, with luck, some basic obedience training. At the time when I was proving that Sam would never make a cattle dog, Tearful and Terrible were about six months old. (These are not usual names, by the way: it was a big litter, and all names had to start with T E. My friend got Teaspoon and Temper.) To anyone used to collies, foxhounds seem totally brainless. They aren't, but their limited intelligence is designed for working within a pack. A single hound sticks close to his master's heels because he fears being left alone or having to make a decision for himself.

Tearful and Terrible followed me about like a couple of substantial and hungry shadows. Forgetting that the huntsman might not thank me, I taught Terrible to retrieve and both of them to fetch the cows. They were slow learners but remembered what they'd been taught. They never learned to nip the cows' heels, but what they lacked in force they made up for with noise. Their yowling sent the cattle running for their lives and the milk yield plummeted.

When the puppies had been returned to the kennels, they both won first prizes in the puppy show. My prize was a gilt powder compact on which was engraved: TEARFUL *** TERRIBLE June 1948. I still have the compact and wonder what a stranger would make of the inscription. I was dogless again, and remained so for some years.

Nowadays, I find myself adopting a lofty attitude towards mongrels. Indeed, some of them *are* ugly, stupid and ill-behaved, but so are some of their blue-blooded owners. Many people who have owned a clever mongrel say, 'All mongrels are clever.' This is like marrying a sincere man and saying 'All men are sincere.' Personal experience isn't always a reliable guide.

In my time, I've owned several mongrels, both clever and thick. Two were among the brightest dogs I've ever known, but their minds didn't work like a collie's. Working dogs are bred to obedience and only anticipate an order in a crisis situation. A working dog which thinks it knows better than its handler is too clever by half, and useless in competition. Better than being stupid, though. . . .

I have told in another book* how I went one day to a farm where I hoped to buy a pony. I bought the pony and asked for a luckpenny. The owner of the pony said, 'I'll give you a luckpenny you'll never forget.' He pointed to a shed whose galvanised door was jammed shut with rocks. 'It's in there,' he said. 'I'm giving you a dog.' He moved some rocks, cautiously opened the door, and called, 'Here, Tiger.'

I waited nervously for a Doberman or Rottweiler to rush out. A tiny straw-coloured puppy emerged unsteadily and stood blinking in the light. His coat handled like poor quality draylon, and he was small enough to sit on the palm of my hand.

*Breakfast the Night Before

When I picked him up, he growled, but I laughed at him and put him in the pocket of my mackintosh. Then I mounted the pony and rode home.

In addition to the raincoat, I was wearing cords, and the type of underwear charitably called 'sensible'. Tiger gnawed his way through the lot and when he reached my leg he kept right on gnawing. When I got home, regretting my bargain, I examined a piece of paper the former owner had given me. It was torn off a letter and had TIGER, written on it – as if I could forget! On the back was printed: Gabriel Aloysius Brook. I have no idea who this fine-sounding person is – or was – and we used to joke about it, saying it was Tiger's showring name.

Tiger grew into a smart little dog, rather like a scaled-down Finnish Spitz. I never discovered what his parentage was, but, in addition to being a discriminating watchdog, he fetched the cows, retrieved small game for my father, and could run down and catch a rabbit in the open. In fact, he combined the best of half a dozen breeds and was an intelligent and always cheerful companion.

I would have expected Tiger to be as faithful as he was clever. When I was away, he sat at the window looking out until I returned and had to be dragged out for walks. He noticed that I picked up any cigarette packets or sweetpapers dropped in the fields and put them in the dustbin. Tiger would spend hours collecting litter while I worked on the farm, and stack it neatly beside the bin. Litter to him meant anything left lying about. When I picked mushrooms, he ran ahead searching, and barked when he found one. When I spent six weeks ill in bed, he fetched boots, shoes and hats to encourage me to get up and go out. Ordered to desist, he levered a book out of the shelf and brought me that instead.

The break-up occurred when Tiger was old and going blind. I got engaged. He refused to be won over by my fiancé; never growling at him, but turning his back and walking away with some dignity. He then transferred his affection from me to my mother, who was delighted. Before, he had accepted her only as a substitute when I was away. I think he was not so much jealous as bitterly offended. Evidently, he thought I was repaying thirteen years of selfless devotion with a shabby trick.

Tiger never relented. For the last two years of his life, he treated my husband and myself alike with polite indifference. I pretended that I didn't mind, but I did.

CHAPTER SIX

THE LIFE OF RILEY

When I got tired of chasing cattle on foot or with a horse, I turned my attention to crops. The war years had seen a boom when you could throw any kind of wheat into a bag and it would end up as flour – optimistically called white. A friend of my mother's was the only person who still had white soda-bread on her table and she explained that her cook sieved the flour. When our cook sieved it the result was beige flour, not white. My mother asked the cook what she sieved it through. 'One of my stockings,' she said.

We had ploughed out a lot of extra land, bought extra horses and paid extra labour in order to produce more wheat. Modern strains of wheat ripen early – haytime and harvest overlap. When I was growing wheat, it ripened in mid-September, or, if the weather was unkind, even later. Stooks could be seen sprouting green ears of corn in the fields in November at times.

In 1958, the year my father died, the summer was one of the worst on record. The farm was understocked, overstaffed and no longer a paying enterprise. I had hastily ploughed out an extra ten acres and sown it with wheat, in order to meet my commitments. It was ready in mid-September, but most of the field was too wet to carry machinery. Many farmers lost all their wheat that year: we would have lost most of ours except for industry born of desperation. Edmund and I scythed the last and wettest two acres, and my mother helped to tie the sheaves. We dragged the sheaves by hand to higher ground, where we could take a trailer without being bogged. Two acres doesn't sound a lot, but it seemed like a whole farm that year.

After the war, the leap into the past was reversed, petrol and oil seemed to return in a flash, along with tea, oranges, coffee and other sorely missed commodities.

Horses disappeared as quickly from the farms as from the roads, and the countryside appeared to sprout little grey Ferguson tractors like mushrooms. By the standards of those days they were fine and I learned to drive a tractor on one of them, lent by a kind neighbour. Another proud owner of a 'Grey Fergie' went so far as to send his pony to the factory and personally chop up his trap for firewood, the very day the first post-war petrol tanker came to town. His action turned out to have been premature. Like thousands of others, his car had been up on blocks in the garage for five years. It refused to start and, when it did, the tyres burst one after another. New tyres had not yet reappeared. We smiled to ourselves as we watched him crossly cycling into town.

Our old Morris had survived better, but mice had eaten the insulation off the wires under the bonnet. My father, always resourceful, separated the bare bits carefully, keeping them apart with non conducting material – sods of turf. Then he drove the car to the garage for servicing. One of the mechanics 'borrowed' the car to go out that night. It stopped and he looked under the bonnet where he was surprised to find a number of sods of turf. He removed these and drove on. Later, he switched on the lights. The explosion that followed sent him careering into a deep ditch. As they say, you can't beat the old horse.

Horses whose owners liked a drink or two regularly found their way home without much help from their drivers. Many of those horses knew which pub to stop at. A farmer from this parish used to spend a considerable amount of time and money at Nolan's Bar to which he drove in a trap drawn by a grey mare, while his wife stayed at home. When this farmer got the 'flu, his wife harnessed the grey mare and drove to town to fetch the doctor. The mare trotted slowly but with determination up to the door of Nolan's Bar, where she stopped. Nothing would induce her to go any farther, and the lady had to leave her there and seek the doctor on foot. Later, after a suitable interval, the mare consented to turn and trot gently home.

I acquired a little car after I had been horse-dealing long enough to pay for it, but a tractor was still vetoed. Neither of the two workmen drove one and neither was young, said my father. True, my horses were paying better than the farm, so my time was better spent at the fairs, but saddle horses are a luxury; I never entirely depended on them.

I borrowed my neighbour's little grey Fergie again and tried to teach Paddy to drive it. He sat on it while I got it started, showed him the controls and got him to press the clutch pedal as I put it in low bottom gear. This would pro- duce a speed of about two miles an hour. I instructed Paddy to raise his foot gently and stood back. With a slight – a very slight – jerk, the tractor moved forward and set off at a crawl. Exclaiming, 'Jesus, Mary and Joseph!' Paddy jumped down and could neither be threatened nor coaxed into getting back in the seat. Eventually, Edmund learned how to drive and he – I can't imagine how – taught Paddy who became a reasonably good driver. He sometimes shouted at the tractor at first, but he never – unlike me – did anything stupid with it.

I couldn't go on borrowing from my neighbours, and my horse-dealing left less and less time for following farm horses, so I decided to hire from the garage. I was the only person insured to drive those hired tractors and there were many occasions when the insurance companies narrowly escaped large claims. Some had no brakes, others had strange steering, the drive shafts were never protected and one of them went on fire twice. (These were minor fires, quenched with a wet sack.)

I remember a huge orange Ford which had to be primed with petrol, poured in out of a jug, and which had only two usable forward gears – bottom and top. As it had no governor, it was possible to drive it at thirty miles an hour along the road. Just a little better was an old, battered David Brown, another big machine. This was the last I hired before buying one of my own. It was a late harvest, before the general use of combines in this area, and we were drawing in the last of the wheat when Ballinasloe fair came round, on the first Sunday in October.

I had been working hard, stooking then pitching corn and, between times, buying and selling horses. I still had some standing wheat and decided to get it combined. Combines were rare, but there was just one, which arrived on Sunday, the fair day. It was hard in those days to get people to work on a Sunday and I had orders for two horses. That day we worked until midnight, and the next I took three loads of corn to town on a borrowed trailer attached to the brakeless David Brown. On both days I took time off for a frantic dash to Ballinasloe – forty miles – and was luckily able to find suitable horses.

I set off with the last load of corn in a great hurry on Monday evening, because the grain merchants' store would soon be closing. The corn was all in bags, and the trailer a flat one, whose drawbar was a length of railway line, rightly discarded. The tractor roared along at a great rate, but steering it was something else. The method was to spin the wheel and wait. Eventually, the cogs would engage with an agonising jolt. After a day of this, one of my wrists swelled so much that I had to cut my shirtsleeve open.

I backed my load into the bay a few minutes before closing time, with apologies. 'Don't hang about, get on with it,' I was told. At that moment, the dodgy piece of railway line snapped and down came the trailer, yards from the intake point and blocking the long alley which was the only way in – or out. I doubt if I have ever been less popular, and it was night again before everything was sorted out. I got a breakdown gang to shift the trailer, drove home in the dark (I need hardly say the tractor had no lights) and went to bed.

Early next morning I returned from the garage with another borrowed trailer, smaller but sounder, and found a customer for one of my Ballinasloe horses having breakfast with my mother while he waited for me. I gave him some sort of show with the horse over a few jumps and he bought it. 'You must have the life of Riley,' he said. 'Nothing to do only canter around on a horse all day.'

I agreed that I had.

Even when I had my own tractor, a new one which cost £660, I remember, my troubles weren't over. This was to some extent my own fault, patience never having been one of my noticeable virtues.

My father having died, I had cut the workforce from three to two and sold twelve bullocks in order to buy that tractor. But I was still the only driver on the place for the whole of that summer. In haytime, I did my best to combine two roles.

I would go to one of the haytime fairs (Kilrush, Spancilhill, Cahirmee and Limerick,) setting off at some unsocial hour, and buy a horse or two. I would arrange for their transport by train or lorry and try to chase up contacts to secure further deals. This would take all morning and sometimes all afternoon as well. Then I would dash home, get the tractor out and cut a field of hay.

I won't forget the day of Kilrush fair, June 10th, a Saturday. I had some early hay, a heavy crop which looked as if it might be hard to save if the weather broke. I was at the fair, ninety miles from home, at 8.30, and bought two horses. When I got home, it was late afternoon and I decided to cut as much hay as I could before dark. It would be ready to turn on Monday. Cutting was slow, as I was still using the old horse-drawn mower, trailing behind the tractor. There was no way of putting it out of gear, so I had to swing round in a circle at the end of every swath. This meant that I was always clogging up the blade with already mown hay and having to disentangle it.

I was nearing the middle of the field – and the end of my task – by around 10.30 p.m. There was a square left to cut no bigger than a large room. I was tearing round to finish it when, with a long whoosh, the air went out of one of the big back tyres. Six rounds left to cut. Saturday night. There was nothing to be done, and the field was at the extreme end of the farm, down by the river.

I jumped off the tractor in a fine rage and kicked the flat wheel as hard as I could. I was wearing sandals and I dislocated my big toe. I had to hop all the way home to my mother, who yanked the toe back into place at once. The pain was astonishing but I hardly had time to feel it before the joint snapped back into position.

My mother was in almost as bad a temper as I was, because the horses had arrived from Kilrush while I was gone, and she didn't know where I was. She was seventy and not in the best of health at the time. When the lorry arrived, she had asked the driver to unload the horses and turn them loose into a stable. He asked her to help. She protested, 'Why don't you unload them yourself?'

'I have only one arm,' said the driver. She looked and saw that he had an empty sleeve pinned to his chest like Nelson's; no artificial limb, no stump. Yet this man went to all the fairs with his lorry and took unbroken colts all over the midlands, the south and the west. How he managed to turn his vehicle and back it into awkward places without power steering, I don't know, but he did manage. My mother was so impressed that she agreed to hold one of the horses for him, but when I hopped home I got a less than sympathetic reception.

My poor mother – she had a lot to put up with. She must have been bored and lonely and I was hardly ever in the house. This was a shame, as she was the warmest-hearted and wittiest person I have ever known. Things improved for her when I got married and didn't have to work on the farm.

One of the harder things she had to bear was my taste in music. Mothers of a later generation had to endure all the varieties of pop and rock. Mine had to put up with Irish traditional music, to which I was addicted. It's heartening to see this music coming back into fashion; it's do-it-yourself music and looked likely to die out at one time. Being force fed with music on radio and TV discourages people from making their own.

From an early age I sensed an association between horses and music. This may have been because Paddy used to sing *The Rose of Mooncoin* as he ploughed, and a poignant ballad called *The Night that Alice Died*. (She fell upon the cold, cold ground and never more did rise.) He sang this when he was happy, saying that it encouraged the horses. Perhaps it did.

I used to visit a neighbour's house where different members of the family played the fiddle, tin whistle and button accordion. We sang loudly, and danced until we knocked sparks out of the flagstones. Often we invented ditties about anything that was happening, making them up as we went along. Then television arrived and singing gave way to watching.

45

Many musicians deserved better instruments. The traditional bodhran, made of a goatskin and played with a bone, could be made locally; but I have seen fiddles made from butter boxes and accordions with half the keys missing in the hands of real musicians.

Co Clare was and is the place for traditional music, and I'll always remember a day I spent horse-hunting there. I went first to a farmer whose house was so close to the sea as to be almost in it. I bought one horse there and another in Kildysart, not far away, several hours later. In the meantime, I'd visited half a dozen other farms, buying nothing but collecting hangers-on who wanted to help. In Kildysart, we were invited in for tea and there was quite a crowd. A sing-song started, but nobody had a musical instrument, so we adjourned to the house of the renowned musician, Mrs Crotty. There were several Crottys there and the kitchen was filled to bursting. It had been raining all day, and we all had wet overcoats and heavy boots. I don't remember any alcohol, but I have never drunk so much tea before or since. We danced, too, as well as the cramped space would allow.

After some time, awash with tea, we piled into two cars – there were seven in my Morris Minor – and went to see an old man who was said to be very ill. The idea was to cheer him up, but I was afraid we might be the cause of his death. Not at all. The old man jumped out of his sickbed and joined the party. This was in Kilfenora, so I was gradually heading in the direction of home. At last we said goodbye. I left my companions to find their way home and set off in the dark. Near Corofin, I had a puncture.

It was still raining hard, and no lights were to be seen. At last I flagged down a car driven by a young man and asked if he could help. 'Of course,' he said, 'I'll lend you a flashlamp.' He handed it through the window, adding, 'Leave it on the wall when you've finished with it,' and waving cheerfully as he drove away. I changed the wheel and drove as far as Killaloe where I had another flat. There

I had to borrow a wheel, but at least I didn't have to change it.

As before, my mother was alone and worried. Two of my musical friends had decided to deliver the horses with their trailer. This wasn't in the contract so it was a nice surprise for me.

'She left an hour before we did,' said Mike, who owned the trailer. 'I wonder where she's got to.'

'I don't know in the face of God,' said Pajoe gloomily.

My mother, more worried still, asked them in for tea. When I arrived, Mike and Pajoe were trying to cheer her up by singing to her. They chose Paddy's favourite, *The Night That Alice Died*. There was relief all round when I appeared and my mother made another pot of tea. Then I fetched my accordion, and the party broke up around one a.m.

It was one of the times when I had serious doubts about whether the day's work would pay. As it happened, the two horses made plenty of profit. In my book they have been given the names: Teaparty and Singalong.

Although horseboxes and lorries were fairly plentiful at this time, most dealers still depended on the railways for carrying horses. There were more trains and more lines open than there are today, and the railway was cheaper than the road. When I started dealing I used to bicycle to the station in the morning, and run my purchases home loose in the evening, riding the quietest while Edmund or Paddy brought up the rear on my bike. No wonder the children of Nenagh ran alongside catcalling and shouting, 'Ride him cowboy', and 'Where are you camping tonight?' The mind boggles when you try to imagine that sort of thing in today's traffic.

'Missing the train' was more than an inconvenience, it could be a disaster or at best a time-consuming nuisance. Riding a fit hunter is a very different thing from riding an underfed three-year-old with one shoe and no mouth. It took me four hours to get one such fifteen miles home, having missed the train. I rode him only because he wouldn't lead.

This was nothing beside the feat of a dealer who rode a horse he had bought from me eighty miles to catch the boat at Waterford. Needing a helper to bring along a second horse, he persuaded a young man who was a sales rep in sewing machines to go with him. This unfortunate youth had no idea what he was letting himself in for. He thought at first he was riding merely to Thurles – then to Cashel – then the truth dawned.

The railways were geared to horses in the fifties. I remember the Dublin express being delayed for some minutes in Nenagh while the blacksmith tacked a shoe on to an equine passenger. Horses travelled slowly, cheaply and uninsured on the goods trains, or in comparative comfort by passenger service. This could still mean a cattle wagon, but it was hitched to the express and the horses were loaded and unloaded on the platform among the passengers.

One such load became involved with a wedding party in North Cork. The party, large, noisy and good-humoured, was gathered round the bridegroom who was trying to lift his bride into the carriage. She, a sturdy young woman, was about double his weight. 'Jesus lads, she's stuck to the ground!' cried the bridegroom as he hauled away. At that moment, two wild young horses broke loose and plunged whinneying through the crowd with halters trailing. The bride screamed; the bridegroom abandoned her and jumped into the train, the crowd scattered. The owner of the horses wandered up remarking, 'Tis ridiculous crowding the platform with people that don't be travelling. Why the hell didn't they stay in the hotel?' He retrieved the horses which a porter had caught in the booking hall and dragged them away.

Horses travelled either loose or in stalls. If the latter, they were chained up in front of cast-iron mangers, looking through hatches to the grooms' compartment. Everything, including the seats, was thickly coated with coaldust.

Before the days of fast food, travelling with horses was a

hungry business. One carried sandwiches (coaldust and ham), or chocolate (fruit, nut and coaldust). One resourceful dealer had an aunt who lived in Portlaoise. As the train drew into the station, she appeared with a plate of unpolluted cold beef which she passed through the window, complete with knife and fork. When he'd finished eating – crossing the Curragh, I think – the ungrateful nephew threw auntie's knife, fork and china plate out of the window. And they say littering is a recent phenomenon.

CHAPTER SEVEN

MUCK AND MONEY

My father's death and the need to pay duty threw me into a frantic scramble to make money. It had been assumed that I would have to sell up, and I was determined not to. But it was an uphill battle.

Let it be clearly understood that I am not a feminist. Some ideas advanced by the earlier woman's libbers were no more than common-sense and don't rightly count as feminism; others would result in women giving up more important rights than equal pay, such as the right to consideration, to being put first and even to tenderness, which I have heard described by an early bra-burner as 'patronising'. However, some of my encounters with male chauvinists in the past did bring out *some* feminist feelings. The bank manager, an excellent man

51

whom I'd always liked, turned into someone quite different when he hid his determination not to allow a woman to borrow behind a sort of little-woman-speak: 'Now we can't have you bothering your little head with that sort of thing. Why don't you get married?' I was big, strong, healthy and reasonably intelligent. I'd been selling horses to the Metropolitan Police, the Household Cavalry and the Swiss Army for several years and had kept myself with the profits. I had a two week holiday every year, owned a reliable car and had bought a thirteen acre field out of profit. I also owned eight horses and six bullocks, which I didn't want to sell before they were ready. But I had to.

The first thing I had to do was to make the cows pay. I'd been separating and churning milk, and selling butter in the shops for years. It was either so plentiful that I couldn't get rid of it or so scarce that there wasn't any going spare to sell. Top price was around 10p a pound. So I invested in three more cows, sold the separator and the churn and started going to the Creamery. I took milk to the Creamery for ten years: a dreadful nuisance, and I couldn't have managed without my mother who took over on horse fair days, but I missed it when I gave it up. The Creamery was an unique kind of social club.

I drove a car with a primitive sort of trailer made out of the body of the gig we drove when the car was laid up. But most farmers in the 'fifties were still using horse- or donkey-drawn carts. We queued up, sometimes for as much as an hour, and people walked around exchanging gossip. Some people arrived with a newspaper, and these were passed around so that everyone could sample them all. Ireland is no longer quite as insular – parochial even – as she was then. I remember the following exchange:

'It says on the paper there was twenty killed in a rail crash.'

'Holy God, that's terrible. Was it in Ireland?'

'No, somewhere in the world.'

Papers read, we waited, patiently or not according to temperament. Once, a fight broke out between a lorry driver and a farmer who had tried to jump the queue. It was a hot day and each was armed with a pound of butter. These were wrapped, to start with, in greaseproof paper. Later, both combatants looked as if they'd been in a custard-pie throwing session. The winner knelt on the loser, rubbing butter on his face and into his hair. Later they went to wash it off, the best of friends again.

When there was nothing like this to enliven the wait, long discussions took place. Purity was a favourite subject – of the milk, I should add. Hygiene wasn't remarkable in the early days. I have seen a child tumble into the milk tank and be fished out again. I have seen a man drop his jacket into the milk, get it out and wring the surplus back into the tank. He was told off for this, but the milk was used. Then progress hit the Creamery, and purity tests began, in the sneaky form of spot checks. Suppliers asked one another anxiously, 'Have you passed your purity test?' Often the reply was a sad shake of the head. But the Creamery officials struggled on, knowing that hygiene at home must be improved too. What of the cat which, pursuing a mouse across a dresser, fell into a pan of cream on a lower shelf? The old lady who owned him lifted him out by the scruff of the neck and squeezed him out like a dishcloth back into the pan. (That didn't happen in Ireland, but in Yorkshire, by the way. I include it for the benefit of all those people who are saying to themselves, 'That could only have happened in Ireland.')

Nearer home, there was the time when I forgot to cover the cream in the dairy at night. In the morning it looked as if there was a pair of grey woollen gloves floating in it . . . which turned out to be fourteen drowned mice. I was about to tip the lot down the drain when a neighbour called. 'Waste is a sin,' she said. 'You should strain it and churn it. Who's to know?'

I hastily threw it away, mice and all, as I suspected she would have accepted it for herself. The woman was horrified. 'I never said you should use it,' she said. 'Sell it. What the eye doesn't see. . . .'

53

As time went on my mother became less keen on going to the Creamery for me, so I had to rely on outside help which wasn't always forthcoming. Neither Edmund nor Paddy could drive a car. I even took the milk to the Creamery on my wedding day, on my way to the hairdresser's. On that occasion though, I was allowed to jump the queue.

Not long before, I'd gone to the Creamery after a late night at a dance, and queued for an hour. Milk was scarce and I had the cans in the boot – or thought I had. When I reached the stand, I discovered the boot was empty, the milk at home. I had to drive back five miles for it, return and queue all over again. That took months to live down: a joke, however feeble, was made to last and last at the Creamery. When some bright lad found a rubber stamp, and stamped the words *export reject* on the manager's white-trousered bottom without being noticed, the story went round with embellishments for weeks.

At this time, the Creamery was next door to a field, now the car park at the cattle mart. A cow lived in this field, and her owner milked her and brought the milk in a churn on the handlebars of his bike. I have also seen him milk her, when she was going dry, in the street. He would take perhaps a quart of milk to the Creamery in a bucket. One day when a number of people were sheltering in my car from the rain, this man passed by driving two bullocks. 'Look at the grand cows, Dada,' piped up a little boy, face pressed to the window.

'They're not cows, they're bullocks,' said Dada. 'Cows is the lads has tits.'

There used to be a busy draper's shop in the town, with a large orchard at the back which had no way into the street except through the shop. The owner thought it a pity to waste the grass, so he bought a heifer calf and carried her through the shop one day, wrapped in a sack, to the orchard. There she lived for many years, growing, not unnaturally, into a cow. Every year, the Artificial Insemination man made his way unobtrusively through the shop; every year, the cow had a calf which was carried out wrapped in a sack, and sold. Every morning, at around 9 a.m., a man emerged from the draper's with a bucket of milk which he carried down to the Creamery. In springtime, two buckets. At last, the man who milked the cow left, and her owner decided to sell her. He thought it would attract least comment if he drove her out through the shop at night, which he did. A party of merrymakers leaving the hotel late, told their friends next day that they'd seen a cow emerging from a draper's shop at three a.m. The advice they got was to take more water with it.

There was a comradeship about the Creamery, of a kind which is less common than it used to be. It was also a link between town and country. A bulk tank is a handy thing, but I'm not the only one who misses the Creamery.

Over the ten years when I was going to the Creamery, a great many farmers acquired cars, but a minority preferred a horse for the purpose. The favoured transport was a flat cart or 'dray car' drawn by a creamery cob.

A creamery cob is, or was, a strong clean-legged animal, anywhere between 14.2 and 15.2 hands high. Ideally, it was sired by an Irish Draught out of a thoroughbred pony cross. This cross could also produce a top-class riding horse, but the true creamery cob wasn't really a riding animal. It had too much action and not enough life about it. Most farmers favoured a mare, with the idea of 'knocking a foal out of her' in her spare time.

Unfortunately, the foaling and calving seasons coincide, and many a mare came to the Creamery almost too wide to fit between the shafts. One of them actually foaled back into the cart she was pulling, a dedicated working mother if ever there was one. I should mention that she was weeks before her time, mares being notoriously bad at reckoning dates.

I once had a day's hunting on a mare known simply as

55

Fogarty's Cob. She could jump like a grasshopper, and almost as suddenly. Standing facing a wooden gate, she abruptly took one step back and jumped over it, dropping her head at once to graze. I turned a backward somersault worthy of a circus act, landing, amazingly, on my feet. Years later, I bought a brown horse I called Fairfax, which made a showjumper for the great Yorkshire dealer, Bert Cleminson. Bert wanted to know more of the horse's breeding and I discovered he was out of Fogarty's Cob.

Dealers looking for riding school horses for the English trade found a rich supply at the creameries of West Clare. Villages like Doonbeg, Moyasta, Cooraclare and many more were full of hardy little animals suitable for beginners to ride. Their great advantage was that they were yoked at two years old, but not asked to do heavy work. They had learned to be biddable before they reached their full strength, were up to weight, and most were well fed and well treated. Dealers buying horses which would never be between shafts again asked, not 'Has he been ridden?' but, 'Do you take him to the creamery?' Hundreds of these cobs were bought over the years by the Doyle brothers from Limerick. They went to various riding establishments in England. I seldom bought an animal of this type, but was often asked to try one out for a buyer, to see how it behaved under a saddle. The best place for this was the old Limerick Haymarket, where there were concrete steps about eighteen inches high. Most of the cobs would literally trot up and down them, as surefooted as goats.

The sudden leap in the cost of transport stopped this trade in its tracks. No more could horses travel in stalls on the boats; it was roll-on roll-off for everything. The cost of container space ate up the profits, since it is a sad fact that a cheap horse takes up as much space as a dear one. Obviously, the cheap ones couldn't pay.

These cobs were useful creatures and are sadly missed. Their hardiness, their versatility and, above all, their temperaments are hard to find today. It would be interesting to know just how many international showjumpers have been bred off members of that endangered species, the creamery cob.

CHAPTER EIGHT

STRUGGLING

After my father's death, as well as going to the Creamery, I tried to increase my cattle herd. It was difficult, given that I couldn't borrow. I used to sell a couple of bullocks for cash, buy a horse with the cash, sell the horse for profit and buy three bullocks with the resulting cheque, thus laboriously acquiring about thirty beasts which didn't appear in my books. This was the only way in which I could get hold of any spending money.

A loan would have paid for them all, and could have been repaid with interest when they were sold, but the bank directors didn't see things this way.

Their mistrust of woman farmers was echoed in Macra na Feirme, an organisation for young farmers. This body ran an agricultural show, where I exhibited young horses once or twice. The standard was low, and they won prizes. These shows were known for running competitions of skill for farmers. One of these was guessing the weight of a heifer for twopence. I proffered two pennies.

'This is just for men and boys,' said the very young man in charge.

'Why?' (I'd been buying cattle for years, and felt better qualified than some of the schoolboys taking part.)

'Because that's the way it is. You can guess the weight of the cake. Or next year, you could go in for baking the best sponge.'

Again I came up against the idea that any man, no matter how thick, automatically knew more about farming than any woman. There was some kind of Divine Right about it. It was many years before this state of things altered, and even now a woman farmer finds it difficult to be taken seriously unless she is known to have a male partner. He may be a drunken layabout; he may have no interest in farming. No matter, he is a man.

The bank manager wasn't alone in thinking that marriage was the only lifesaver for a woman with a farm. My neighbours too had a keen interest in my future (or the future of my land) and constantly suggested suitable partners. They succeeded only in making me suspect the motives of every suitor who came my way.

Two neighbours came rushing up to me at a cattle fair one day, both talking at once. They had, they said, found just the husband for me. A Protestant and, they were almost sure, an orphan.

'You wouldn't want some bitter old grave-dodger living with you,' they said.

I asked anxiously if they had told this paragon of their plans. They hadn't, but thought he would welcome the idea. 'He's not too old,' said one. 'And he has his own teeth.'

Even this wasn't enough for me. They went away, disappointed.

When I did marry, years later, I had to learn to cook almost from scratch. I was fortunate indeed to have six stepdaughters to teach me.

When I was growing up, we always had a cook: not necessarily a good one – some of them were appalling – but a person capable of putting some kind of meal on the table at stated intervals. By degrees, they disappeared, and outside help took their place. I was sixteen when the last one departed. There followed an interval of hunger and indigestion. My mother could make only cakes, which she did excellently; my repertoire consisted of porridge and scrambled eggs; my father could make soup and curry, and, on the cook's night out, he did this. For the purpose of cooking, he first put on his hat – I don't know why. As a rule it was a sign that he was going to do something fairly dramatic.

I remember a dinner party when I was a tiny child and supposed to be in bed. There were, I knew, silver dishes with bonbons in them on the dinner table, so I slipped down to help myself, but I'd chosen the wrong moment. I heard the gong and immediately afterwards the dining room door opened. I dived under the table where I lay, along with my mother's dog, for the whole of the meal.

There was a large and probably valuable mahogany sideboard in the dining room, on which stood a huge, heavy silver tray. (Both sideboard and tray are gone long since.) During that dinner the tray suddenly crashed down, sending a number of smaller silver objects flying off the sideboard. Some rolled under the table, but luckily nobody looked for them there. My father got up and left the room. When he returned, he was carrying a hammer and wearing his hat. He then hammered a two inch nail into the sideboard and stood the tray up again, leaning it against the nail; after which he removed his hat and went on with his meal.

Before our first cookless Christmas, my parents anxiously

discussed the preparation and cooking of a turkey. 'Surely it can't be difficult,' I said.

'You do it then,' was the answer to that, so I was relieved not to be at home on Christmas Eve.

My mother had bought a bird which was supposed to be oven-ready. 'Why, it's even been stuffed,' she exclaimed in delight. Alas, it was nature's own stuffing, and I returned to find my father (wearing his hat) disembowelling the turkey over the sink with the help of a toasting fork, of all things. We had soup, curry and cake for our Christmas dinner, but my father wasn't quite beaten. He hacked the bird in pieces which we ate, first baked and later curried, for days.

The next year, we decided that a goose might be easier to deal with. I went off for a very long ride while my parents prepared it, feeling that three in the kitchen would be a crowd. The goose was too long for the oven, so my father, always resourceful, cut through its breastbone with a hacksaw and bent it into a V shape. The end product looked curious but tasted fine.

In time, my mother learned how to scramble eggs and I mastered soup and curry, but the Christmas dinner remained a toss-up for years; a gamble with an element of surprise. We amassed dozens of books of recipes, but somehow there was always something burned, something forgotten.

I discovered an ancient journal of my great-great-grandmother's, a lady who lived in England almost two hundred years ago, the wife of a clergyman and the mother of several hungry sons. With a nib hardly broader than a hair, she sets out the menu for a 'breakfast for one hundred hungry soules'. It consisted of turkeys, geese, hams, venison pasties, mutton pasties, game pie, twenty gallons of the best beef broth and two gross of jellied hard-boiled eggs. There was much more which I've forgotten, and the ale was measured in barrels. I think this must have been a hunt breakfast and, if it was immediately followed by the hunt, those hungry hunters must have been martyrs to ulcers and indigestion. At all events, this section is followed by a list of fearful sounding remedies for 'biliousness and colicky humours'.

Great grandmama interlarded her recipes with notes about how the meal had been received. 'William left his food upon his plate, but I think he may be in love.' 'Mince pyes are sure to please. I used 2 pounds of neat's tongues parboyled and pealed, 4 pounds of good beef suett, the same of raisons, pruens and currans, 4 large Pippens, spice, verjuice and sack. I used orange, limmon and citron peal candid. The pyes did vastly please the men, who fell asleep thereafter and snored mightily.' Some of the recipes required two or three gallons of cream, a couple of dozen eggs and a firkin of butter. Did cholesterol affect hearts in the eighteenth century? The lady lived on until her hundredth year, and all her household survived into old age.

One of the recipes is for 'umbel pie,' the dish which gave rise to the saying 'to eat humble pie.' Umbels were the heart liver and entrails of a deer, and traditionally the huntsman's perks. While the aristocracy dined on venison, the huntsman and his family ate umbel pie. Great great grandmama's umbel pie, surprisingly, seems to have been a sweet dish, using much the same ingredients as the mince pyes, plus 'thrice the weight of the umbels in sugar.' Ugh.

My ancestress ran into difficulties in Lent, when her clergyman husband decreed that the whole household should 'abjure the fleshe of beastes for forty days, while pondering on the temporary nature of human life.' Undaunted, his wife fed him on 'mince pyes without fleshe.' 'For these,' she tells us. 'I boyled ten eggs very hard and minced them with a pound of suett and a pound of currans. I then added nutmeggs, cinnamon and rosewater. The pyes sufficed the three men adequately, as I followed them with a bag pudding. In future, I will allow six eggs for eache.'

It is a pity that the original journal has been lost, so that all I have now are the parts of it copied by my mother.

As I went to more and more fairs, in search of both cattle and horses, I found less time to spend at home. The horses were paying for the losses made by the farm over a period of years, as well as keeping my mother and myself in comfort if not in luxury. Gradually, the farm too began to make a profit and I applied for a grant to reclaim and drain seventy acres. Around that time, I fell downstairs and seriously damaged my back.

The months that followed were both worrying and painful. I went around in a plaster cast for four months, spent six weeks in hospital and began to wonder if I was in the wrong profession. I was obliged to spend several hours a day lying flat on my bed, chafing at the thought of all the things I should have been doing. I took up Aran knitting professionally, and used the time to knit endless sweaters, the cable needle held between my teeth, but this didn't soothe my nerves. It was time to make a decision.

I could delegate farm work as, by then, Paddy and Edmund were capable tractor drivers. But I couldn't delegate my horse-dealing. I bought a horse or two from people I trusted, sight unseen, and there wasn't anything wrong with them; but they were bought too dear, there was no room for commission for my agents and profit for me. I left my knitting and went back to the horse fairs, cross-eyed with painkillers.

There came a time when I didn't think I could carry on, and didn't even want to. That was when I advertised the farm for sale. The year was 1961, and the asking price for my two hundred and four acres was £12,000. However, nobody was tempted, and £10,000 was my best offer. I might even have taken it, but for a salutary lesson I learned at the time.

One of my buyers owned a pub. He was most anxious to buy a farm and had been saving up for years. It was he who had offered £10,000. One evening, this man, whom I will call Chris, turned up at my house with a suitcase and asked to see me privately. I took him into the dining room and he put his case down on the table and started trying to persuade me to accept his price for the land.

I listened fairly patiently, but said at last, 'No, I've told you I won't take ten thousand – or eleven. Twelve is the price.'

'I'll make you take ten,' said Chris. 'You won't be able to say no.' With that, he opened the suitcase with a flourish and stood back. A powerful smell of stale stout and cheap pipe tobacco filled the room. The case was stuffed with five pound notes. And yes, there was £10,000 there. Chris invited me to count it, but I declined.

I thought about the fields, the garden, the house where I'd always lived, and I looked at the mound of grubby fivers which Chris was eagerly showing me. I said, 'I've changed my mind about selling. I'll take the place off the market tomorrow.'

Chris was put out. He argued. He offered another £200. I stood firm. As I was going to bed that night, it struck me that it was some while since I had noticed my back. It had become less painful. I'm still here.

The lesson is too obvious to need underlining, but it has stood me in good stead. I no longer thought of market price, but of real values.

I became even more aware of such values when I started keeping sheep soon afterwards. A field of standing wheat has already cost money. It will take a lot more money to convert it into loaves of bread. A failed crop can be a disaster, leaving the farmer with unpayable debts. If you own a few sheep and prices collapse, you have options. You can sell your cull ewes for what they'll fetch, having collected all available subsidies, and keep your ewe lambs for breeding instead. If you can't sell your wether lambs, you can eat them – or somebody else can. They can be killed and frozen and, even if they are silly cheap, you can replace them with breeding females equally cheaply. Having bought good quality ewes, you sit tight and await better things. A lamb sold for £70 in a flying trade is no better to eat than a similar lamb worth £30 when trade is flat. The fact that an animal was expensive won't make it provide any extra dinners. A fat sheep or

65

a fat bullock is a solid reality, easily converted into food. That's more than can be said for the mucky tokens we call money.

CHAPTER NINE

FOOLS RUSH IN

I t's amazing that I've managed to write eight chapters about my life, with only a passing reference to sheep. They have been part of the scenery for so long that I find it hard now to imagine farming without them. Yet I didn't have any until a year after I had made the fateful decision to stay put.

I had been milking cows for almost as long as I could remember. The herd now numbered fifteen. My first creamery cheque was for just over nine pounds, but now it averaged around £50 a month. Not riches, but enough – just – to get by. The cows did badly, and it was a long time before I discovered why: although I liked buying and selling cattle, I hated cows. I thought they were noisy, messy, smelly, stupid creatures, and I liked them even less in busy times like harvest, when I often had to milk them all by hand, as we didn't have a machine.

Sometimes I milked them on Sundays, but Paddy normally did this. He was a ploughman, not a cowman, and did it out of kindness, often after a hurling match. On these occasions, he would lead his bike by the handlebar rather than risk riding it, and wear his cap over one ear. He would sing as he milked, the same sad songs that put energy into the plough-horses. One evening after a particularly good match, I went out to help Paddy milk – I'd seen him reeling across the yard, swinging the buckets and singing tunelessly.

'Did we win, Paddy?' I asked him.

'No, we lost,' Paddy replied carefully. 'That's why I'm worse than I am,' he added.

'I'll milk one of those cows,' I reached for a bucket.

'I have them all milked.'

'Not this one. Look, she's full of milk.' The cow had lately calved and her udder looked likely to burst.

Paddy focussed rather glassily. 'Oh God,' he said. 'I must have milked one of the others twice.'

Paddy and I agreed about cows, but Paddy didn't much like calves either. There was a kind of gloomy 'I told you so' satisfaction about him if one of them died. When Edmund was ill and Paddy was in charge of the cows and calves, he refused to help with anything that was sick. I remember him saying of a sick heifer, 'If she gets well, the best she can do is grow into a cow.' She didn't get well; she died. We had in those days to hand in all ear tags off dead animals, and I asked Paddy to secure the tag before the huntsman arrived to collect the carcase. Later, I was having breakfast when Paddy came in and remarking, 'Here's the tag,' dropped something black, hairy and cold beside my plate. The tag being firmly attached, he had cut off the ear instead.

I bought my first sheep in the face of opposition from both Paddy and Edmund, and much good advice from my neighbours. It was impossible to breed sheep at Crannagh, they said. The lambs would die. And for all I knew they were right: I had no experience of sheep whatever; I had no sheds; I had no dog, no proper fences, and no sense. In addition, I couldn't find any books on the subject and the farming papers were interested only in cows. But all the same I went ahead and bought ten ewes.

I was bewildered by the old wives' tales which abounded at the time. For example, was my neighbour joking when he warned me against cutting the lambs' tails? The good would run out of them by way of the stumps, he said, and they'd never thrive. (This was a warning which I disregarded from the first.)

My ten ewes lambed in a twenty acre field with huge thorny hedges, and I inspected them at midnight and five a.m. with a flashlamp. Naturally, I had no enclosure where I could catch a sick ewe, and wouldn't have known what to do for her anyway.

Edmund had a fund of tales and cures which were of little practical use. When the first ewe lambed, he made collars of red tape for the lambs. 'Why?' I asked.

'The first lambs. It's always been done. It's lucky.'

'Yes, but why?'

'Because that's the way it is.'

I suspect the practice goes back to pagan times. Perhaps it averts the evil eye or propitiates the gods. Another practice I wouldn't countenance was that of draping the afterbirth over a hawthorn tree. (The afterbirth used to be called the 'haw'.) This unpleasant idea must surely have had to do with the may-tree as an emblem of fertility. Anyway, I put my foot down and had the afterbirths buried. Nobody was surprised when almost half of the lambs died. The vet diagnosed lamb dysentery, I gave injections and from that day most survived, but Edmund wasn't convinced.

The weather turned cold in the second half of March and I considered bringing the ewes and lambs into the farmyard. But how to feed them? It was patiently explained to me that sheep wouldn't eat hay, and Providence had never intended them to eat meal. Grass or turnips – nothing else. I hadn't any turnips left, so I tried them with oats and they loved it. I was surprised to hear that sheep didn't drink any water and, for a day or two, I didn't offer them any. Then I began to wonder what they used for making milk and decided that a bucketful couldn't do any harm. Poor things, they mobbed me for it, and I put a trough in their shed. 'They'll die,' said Paddy. On the contrary, they did better than before.

In due course, my sheep were shorn, and I found out why two of them hadn't lambed. They were wethers. Wool was dear that year, so dear in fact that a fleece was sometimes worth more than the sheep wearing it, and the ten fleeces made £30. Ten fleeces this year would hardly make ten pounds, but wages were a fiver a week then and way over £100 now.

'I think I should have a sheepdog,' I said.

'Dogs upset sheep. They sling their lambs and get on their backs and die.'

This information came, of course, from someone who'd never seen a good or even moderate dog at work. Nothing, but nothing, could have been more upsetting to a sheep than Paddy and me practising a bit of midwifery. 'We landed him,' said Paddy, wiping his hands and looking proudly at the limp lamb. The ewe was firmly held down by a knee on her neck, I was trying to make the lamb suck. All this was after I'd run down the ewe, caught her and had an all-in wrestling match which I won by a narrow margin. I took a turn at holding the ewe down while Paddy stood bent double and milked her into the lamb's mouth. The ewe bleated and struggled as hard as she could. The ram I'd bought (for ten sheep, two of them wethers!) hearing one of his wives in trouble, attacked Paddy from behind, hitting him fair and square. I looked up and saw Paddy riding away on the ram's back, still grimly clutching the lamb. He was carried quite a distance before he fell off. After that, I had to deal with newborn lambs unassisted.

I sold my first crop of lambs well. I was horsedealing full-time as well as keeping cattle and growing crops, so I didn't want extra breeding ewes. The handful I had then cost me more headaches than the three hundred and fifty I eventually kept. So I went to a fair and bought sixty lambs. I think my guardian angel was working overtime that day; I knew less than nothing about store lambs. They doubled their money off grass.

My next deal was less lucky. The sheep fair clashed with the horse fair at Ballinasloe, which I couldn't afford to miss, so I sent Edmund to buy lambs for me. He was anxious to buy good ones and afraid of the consequences if he didn't, so he bought from my cousin, thinking to please me. My cousin knew less, if possible, about sheep than I did, and was making his first and last foray into sheepkeeping.

The twenty lambs were Border Leicester crossed with some-thing even larger – perhaps those outsized animals which used to be found in Roscommon and nowhere else. I turned them out on new grass and they grew – and grew. When they were about as big as donkeys, some nine months later, they still weren't fat. I took them to the mart which had just replaced the fair. They could easily have stepped out of their pen. So enormous were they that several people asked me what the new breed was called. After answering truthfully for a while, I told somebody they were called Polled Flockmasters. I got a good price and found out afterwards that word had gone round that Polled Flockmasters were the sheep of the future.

I kept clear of sheep until the following spring, when I took fifty lambs belonging to a neighbour to eat turnips for £15 a month. After a time it occurred to me that if there was room for him to make a profit after paying rent, I should be making it. So I bought the sheep and my neighbour was pleased because they were, he said, getting too fat. There turned out to be a reason for this. Nearly all of them were in lamb and the lambs survived. My neighbour had to take a lot of slagging from his friends about that.

71

My unluckiest purchase was made when I was on a holiday in Connemara. I bought twenty fine big hogget ewes off a mountain near Oughterard, encouraged by a tempting price. I noticed they had rudimentary horns. 'I'd like them better without the horns,' I said.

'There's no extra charge for them,' said the farmer.

I took the sheep home and turned them into a small well-fenced paddock with a rick of hay in it. In the morning, they were marching about on top of the rick, which was, I suppose, the nearest they could get to a mountain. I went to get a ladder to chase them down, carelessly leaving the gate open. When I got back, they'd gone.

I knew nothing of the homing instinct of mountain sheep. They had set off for their native Connemara, always travelling by road and always in the right direction. They did this again and again, and each time I recovered them there was one less than before. When the number was down to seventeen, I sold the rest at a loss.

Keeping sheep efficiently is an all-the-year-round task. The myth persists that 'lambing time' is a nightmare, reminiscent of an emergency ward after a cosmic disaster. For the rest of the year, sheep and shepherd recover from the experience. I've often been asked how I fill my time when lambing's over and 'there's no work with the sheep'. There's always work with sheep, but if you like them, you don't mind. I did mind, very much, working a seven day week with cows.

My husband, John, wasn't a sentimental man, but like me he loved sheep and sheepdogs. He would glance at one of a hundred ewes and say, 'She's carrying dead lambs,' or 'She's getting pneumonia,' or 'She's going to die.' He was always right; the ewe that was going to die always did. I would make a fuss and insist on the vet being fetched, but a sheep which has made up its mind to die usually does. John couldn't explain how he knew these things, but by degrees I learned to

72

recognise them myself – I don't know how. It's more a matter of sympathy than knowledge.

Sympathy and sentiment are, of course, different things. Sentiment is the emotion felt by two families who swap pet lambs before killing and eating them. You couldn't possibly eat dear little Rambo, could you? But your friends could, and you could eat their pet. I also knew two families who swapped rabbits they couldn't bear to kill.

I remember seeing a little boy carrying a black rabbit down the street. Another boy joined him and asked, 'Are you going to eat him?'

'I'm going to keep him, you bloody cannibal,' was the reply. Sentiment of a kind, but understandable.

I was as sentimental as the next when I started breeding sheep, there being something which appeals to one's maternal instinct about an abandoned lamb. Agnes was a typical case. I found Agnes, abandoned by her mother, in a ditch. I brought her back to life against all the odds, spending most of a night feeding her with warm milk, drop by drop. Agnes was a short-backed, tubby lamb, of mixed ancestry, and the best place for her would have been the freezer. I was well aware of this, but I stubbornly kept her for breeding. Agnes produced one short-backed, tubby lamb every year until she, providentially, died.

A farmer of my acquaintance kept a pet lamb for eleven years – when toothless, she lived mainly in the kitchen and ate porridge among other things. But, unlike Agnes, she was a fine specimen and a prolific mother.

Sympathy is nursing a sick animal – and knowing when to give up. Sentiment is keeping a poor old horse turned out in a field all the year round without company or care, because you can't bear to put him down: which is not kindness but cruelty.

I'm sure that when you start thinking of farm animals as 'stock units' you lose touch with reality. It may be all right if you deal in thousands; in a small enterprise it's a mistake.

As I write this, my ewes are lambing; it's midnight, time for a last visit to the shed. There the lights are on and the sheep are lying down asleep. As I walk among them, hardly any bother to get up. I talk quietly to them, which may be silly but does no harm and may do good.

I have the same sympathy with horses, dogs, even bullocks, but not cows. Accordingly, all cows treat me with suspicion. If you have to deliver a calf or lamb, the task is much easier if the mother trusts you, because she will relax. Some vets inspire trust in their patients, just as some doctors do; others don't.

You have to like sheep to put up with them, as they can try your patience to the last. Highest in irritation value comes the lamb which can, but won't suck; this is followed by the ewe which could, but won't get up. Almost as bad is the lamb which jumps straight back into the bramble filled ditch you've spent half an hour getting him out of.

It's obvious that mutual understanding and trust are important for a dog and his master. I believe they can be developed between shepherd and sheep to the advantage of both.

CHAPTER TEN

FUND-RAISING

One of my reasons for branching out into sheep keeping was to lessen the work for myself. I had been told by a doctor in England that I was unlikely to be able to lead an active life following my back injury. Fortunately, he was wrong – those sheep would have discovered any weak spots. They took twice as much care as the cattle, mainly because of my abysmal ignorance.

Although I continued to ride the horses I was selling, I did so more cautiously, and I practically gave up hunting. For some time, I kept going, too proud to admit that I was frightened as well as in considerable pain. Then a fellow dealer put it to me that hunting, for me, was like jumping a fixed post and rails when the gate was open – stupid.

My hunting being confined to North Tipperary, with brief visits to Galway and Limerick, I was constantly told that things were very different in England. Spit and polish, tradition gloriously upheld – it didn't sound too cheerful. I had been secretary for some time to the local hunt, a farmer's pack notably lacking in spit and polish. Yet, when I went out on foot with an English pack run by farmers in Yorkshire, it was remarkably like home. A fierce argument broke out at the meet over the sale of a horse, my host wore a felt hat and wellies, the hunt terrier had a bloody fight with a pet dog a lady had brought with her on a lead, there was talk of barley and silage. Just like home.

Our only concession to Tradition with a capital T was our fieldmaster, a man who was a stickler for etiquette, sadly out of place in North Tipperary. He would lecture the children at the meets (who didn't listen, anyway.) 'You must treat the master with due respect at all times,' he said. 'Remember he comes second only to God.'

> In the year of Our Lord, twenty-seven
> I used to go out with the Quorn
> I knew I was nearer to Heaven
> Than those who were lowlier born.
> For the Master himself once addressed me,
> 'Go to hell, you unprintable sod!'
> His command of the language impressed me
> For I knew he came second to God.
>
> I used to go out with the Cottesmore
> When I was a sub in the Blues –
> I was owing my tailor and lottesmore
> And hadn't a whole lot to lose . . .

I don't remember all of this ditty, but it ended:

> . . . A person of breeding and merit,
> A credit to good mastership

He sleeps with four dogs and a ferret
While his wife goes to bed with the whip.

And now that the matter is reckoned,
I've come to the end of my song –
Put God first and your MFH second
And you'll never go very far wrong.

Spit and polish can be carried to extremes. I think this may
be a legacy from the days when a high proportion of masters were army officers, and from the traditional connection
between hunting field and battlefield.

There was, and in some places still is, a belief that an army
or ex-army man is the most suitable person to fill the post of
MFH, Pony Club instructor or showing judge. Okay if the
man has hunting or jumping experience, but hard to explain
if he is familiar only with tanks. I suppose the idea persists
because of the long history of horses in the army, although
most had been replaced by armoured vehicles fifty years ago.

It is a fact that many men have joined the British Army
because of a love of horses. I find this hard to understand.
Horses have always suffered hideously in war. Some leader
observed that you could ride your horse as long as it was
mobile, shelter behind it when it was down and eat it when
it was dead. Perhaps he was a horse lover, perhaps merely
practical.

When I ceased to be of much value as a whipper in, I
was much in demand for organising fund-raising events.

All sorts of difficulties beset the hunt committee, and most
of them were to do with finding things. These things included
foxes, masters, new subscribers and cash. When, after a long
search, a master was found, money had to be raised to pay
his guarantee, and I was put in charge of running dances.

There can hardly be a less profitable event than a hunt dance, described as a 'social' in order to avoid paying entertainment tax. These socials were by invitation only, so they involved a great deal of work, including the making of huge piles of ham sandwiches and handing round of same. The committee of eight rapidly dwindled to three, at which stage we rebelled. The socials were reduced from six to two a year, which was plenty.

The fashionable way to raise money today is by sponsorship, but that hadn't been thought of at the time. You can find sponsors for almost any activity now. Hunt personnel try to persuade each other to sponsor their children to ride somewhere at so much a mile. Of course, if you can interest the media, you might find someone willing to sponsor you to ride from Cork to Belfast on a donkey or in a pram. This is true dedication.

Another time-honoured way of making money is the raffle or draw. Selling tickets is a poor way of making friends – in fact you lose the friends you already have – but it is probably the most reliable way of raising cash, provided that enough thick-skinned ticket-sellers can be found. I organised a raffle for a pony once. Members felt that it wouldn't pay, and I was allowed hunt funds to pay for the pony only on condition that I guaranteed to sell enough tickets to cover the outlay. This took less than a week.

One of the other prizes was a sheepdog puppy. I had to promise this before it was born, but – disaster – it died at a week old. This meant that I had to ring up other breeders until I found a replacement, and pay for it. Then the businessman who won it asked for cash instead. I paid him. Meanwhile, I was trying to find a customer for the puppy. As it wasn't my own breed, my customers preferred to wait for the next litter. The puppy was six months old before I found a home for him. And I'd named him Lucky.

In the interval between the death of my own puppy, and the purchase of Lucky, I was trying to sell a ticket to a farmer. He asked about the pup, and I began to say that it had died and I was getting another. He interrupted furiously before the second part of the message: 'I didn't think you were sunk so low that you'd try to sell tickets for a dead dog!'

The hunt ball was a much better money-spinner than the old socials, but involved a lot more outlay. The socials were held in a gloomy upstairs hall where the paper chains were never taken down for reasons of economy. During the more vigorous dances, the floor would shake alarmingly, dislodging flakes of plaster and cobwebs from the ceiling of the room below. We used to wonder seriously if it might give way. As money was our motive, we crammed as many bodies as we could into the room, and it was probably a good thing that the insurance regulations were tightened up. Hunt balls were held in hotels, so were normally downstairs, but even they had unforeseen risks.

The hunt chairman at one time was a bank official: a rather fussy man who liked things to be just so. He can't have been much more than five feet tall, and was known for his meticulous dress and for his insistence that everybody behave nicely. He and I were an ill-matched pair on the dance floor.

The hunt ball was in the Lakeside Hotel at Killaloe, and the windows opened onto the garden. As we waltzed by the window, the sash was pushed up from outside, and blurred but truculent voices demanded entry at half price because the dance was half over. My partner, courteous as always, bent down to explain politely why this was impossible. He was immediately seized by the collar and dragged halfway through the window. I grabbed his coat tails and shouted for help; two men came to my assistance just as the coat began to split at the waist. The secretary and I then caught hold of a leg apiece and hauled the poor gentleman to safety, minus his white tie. After that, the windows were kept bolted.

It is a tradition here to hold the hunt ball on New Year's

Eve. One of my earliest memories is of my parents setting off for the ball dressed in white tie and tails (him) and apricot taffeta (her). My nurse said when they'd gone, 'You won't see them again till next year.' Although the feeble joke was soon explained – it was only a few hours to midnight – the feeling of alarm stayed with me for ages.

As I grew older, and the apricot taffeta got shabbier, I used to envy my parents profoundly. I imagined something like the ballroom scene in the first film I ever saw; some Viennese soufflé with Nelson Eddy in it. Chandeliers, champagne, beautiful people, beautiful dresses, an orchestra playing the Blue Danube, romantic moments in the moonlit conservatory. I asked questions and discovered that the Hunt Ball wasn't at all the fairytale event I'd imagined. At that time, it took place in an ice-cold upper room in the Courthouse. On one occasion, a lady put her foot through a rotten floorboard, and the hole was still there the following year. The year after that, it was patched with the lid of a biscuit tin. After one of these events, my parents stayed overnight in an even icier place, a huge, freezing mansion called Traverston. They huddled, shivering in the kitchen, warming their hands in their coat-sleeves because the drawing room fire had gone out.

'What about a nightcap?' said their host.

What a brilliant idea! They accepted eagerly, and were rewarded with tepid Ovaltine and stale cream crackers.

About fifteen years later, I inherited my mother's apricot taffeta, and set off for my first ever hunt ball, which was also my first proper dance. I was nineteen, and was odd woman out, having been invited along by a married couple.

There was a dinner party first, where I sat between a stone deaf man of about eighty and a totally silent elderly woman. I was afraid that, if I ate much, my dress would burst, as I was two stone heavier than my mother and ten inches taller. However, I couldn't resist chocolate sauce with my ice cream, and poured it on with a liberal hand. Alas, it was brown gravy, which should have been removed with the joint. My companions either didn't notice or pretended not to. In the end, I ate hardly anything, but I split the dress anyway.

Many years afterwards, I attended a hunt ball in Limerick where, by an oversight, soup was served at the end of the meal instead of coffee. I'd been having an argument with my partner who was still huffy. When I remarked, 'That's soup, not coffee,' he replied, 'Rubbish.' Mind you, it was the sort of Oxo consommé that isn't unlike black coffee to look at. My partner put a spoonful of sugar in his mug, stirred it and took a generous swallow. I managed not to gloat too much. That particular dance was an all time low as far as catering was concerned. We'd had to queue for the best part of an hour for plastic ham on paper plates, soggy salad and the soup/coffee.

One hunt ball which probed the depths was held in the Scout's Hall in Nenagh in the early fifties. The band we'd engaged was run by Rinty Monaghan, a boxer, and was unusually expensive. Rinty shadow-boxed while his band performed and they were immensely popular. However, they didn't turn up until one a.m. having been engaged for nine thirty. In the long, cold interval, a lady played the piano and some of us sang.

When I started going out, dress dances in the country were commonplace. The country-house hunt ball could be wonderful or awful, depending on the band, the host, the finances of the hunt and, above all, the heating. One which I attended took place in a vast house heated only by a few – a very few – oil stoves, dotted about in the immense rooms. They were as dangerous as they were inefficient. At another dance, where the catering was by the ladies' committee, the ladies concerned almost came to blows and had to be separated.

When dress balls gave way to dinner dances, and dinner dances gave way to discos, the old timers made some concessions to changing times, but not many. I remember a keen hunting man who never went to any other kind of dance, his scarlet coat reeking of mothballs, obstinately waltzing to whatever music the disco had to offer. I was sorry for his partner, who was showing signs of desperation, but the old man seemed perfectly happy.

Anybody who thinks that Molly Keane's marvellous description of a hunt ball in *Good Behaviour* is exaggerated can take it from me that they're wrong. It's understated if anything. Hunt balls are the only social occasions where such snippets of conversation can be heard as 'How are you off for flesh?' 'The new draft seem a nice, level lot,' or 'Her eyes are brighter today, but her legs are still puffy.' This refers of course to the owner's mare, not his wife.

At these functions, respectable citizens may blow hunting horns, whoop, holloa and dance on tables. The odd thing is, that often quite old people are the most childishly happy. Perhaps it's because they go out less often than their children – and grandchildren.

'Can you hold them back for another five minutes?' asked an anxious lady, sheltering behind a stack of cardboard boxes.

'We'll do our best,' gasped the two strong men, specially trained for the job. Angry muttering and an occasional yell came from the struggling mob outside the double doors.

No, it wasn't the end of a siege, although the ladies in the village hall were in some physical danger. When the doors burst open on the stroke of three, the customers surged into the hall where a jumble sale in aid of the hunt was being held, back in the 'fifties.

The crowd descended as one man (or woman) on the stalls where jam and homemade cakes were displayed. These were cleared in seconds, and the buyers converged on the clothes counter. The counters were trestles, wobbly trestles at that. The buyers were so eager, the bargains so good, that they forced the trestles back against the wall. The sellers, including myself, were in some danger of being cut in half. One old man, who never missed a sale, bought all the shirts on offer, regardless of size, price or style. His methods of getting to the front were, I suppose, no less crude than those of many a London commuter in rush hour. He called these events 'jungle sales', a good name for them. Everything was sold within an hour, and we counted up a heartening amount of money before going home to recover.

People who should have known better often sent in stuff which should have gone straight into the dustbin. We dumped these offerings out of sight. A friend of mine, a tireless organiser, told me proudly that she had been promised a fur coat for the sale by a well-to-do lady. The coat arrived on the morning of the sale in a large cardboard box. It smelled of camphor and – something else? We lifted it up cautiously, and maggots rained out of it. My friend crammed the coat back into the box and ran with it, shuddering, to the yard behind the hall where we doused the lot with paraffin and burned it.

I priced jumble all morning, but had to be absent from the sale. I called to help clean up when it was over, and met my friend, looking shaken. 'The owner of the coat's just been in,' she said. 'She asked how we'd got on with it.' There was still a powerful reek of paraffin and burning musquash in the area.

'My God! What did you say to her?'

'I told her it was the very first thing to go. Luckily she was in a hurry, she went off all smiles.'

The sales have calmed down since then. There are more chain stores offering low-priced goods, and it is positively chic to patronise second-hand and swap-shops. Jumble sales are no longer actually dangerous.

As we on the Hunt committee struggled to make money, we read in the sporting papers about rich packs in England and their foot-followers' clubs. These amassed large amounts of money, and spent it on hunt horses, trailers, Land Rovers and oil paintings of retiring masters. Our own foot-followers were people who had fallen off their horses. Following by car never caught on – the hedges are too high and the country too hilly to keep in touch. There was no money to buy as much as an extra tin of paint in those days.

Many and long were the committee meetings organised to generate fresh ideas. Sometimes they went on into the small hours. Often tempers were lost. The meetings were held in a lounge bar; a warm, comfortable haven. Regular patrons had to drink elsewhere.

I particularly remember an occasion when our concern was even more than usually skint. We were arguing for and against paying into an emergency fund. Suddenly the door opened and a very drunk man appeared, staggered into the middle of the room and looked glassily round. 'Any of you lads lend me a tenner?' he asked hopefully, and fell flat on his face. There were no volunteers. A couple of heavies arrived and took him away, and we continued as if nothing had happened.

Soon a violent argument broke out. One by one, the committee members threatened to resign, and finally did so, en bloc. We all then retired to the saloon bar to discuss the matter in depth. After an hour or two, we re-elected ourselves, returned to the lounge and wound up the meeting. We all parted the best of friends, around two a.m., and the financial situation was saved by the usual whip round.

I was secretary at that time, a job I relinquished with no regret. In fact, as my back improved and my horse-dealing business grew, I had less and less time for other things.

CHAPTER ELEVEN

FROM POINT TO POINT

Not all ways of raising money were unpleasant for the sponsors; the point to point was generally enjoyed by everybody, although ours was held for years in February and beset by problems of bad weather.

The first point to point I remember was in – I think – 1935. I was holding my nurse's hand and we were running in order, she said, to see someone killed. There was a race in progress, and the field was approaching a notorious double bank with a deep drain on either side. We arrived panting, and joined the crowd waiting hungrily for thrills and spills. I can recall waving legs as horses rolled on the ground, but nobody was killed that day.

Point to pointing in Ireland in the thirties was like the

cross-country section of a three day event done on half-fit horses and with no safety regulations or rules. Much of the course was out of sight of the crowd, and once round was the rule. 'Out in the country' weights could be handed to a friend, to be collected on the way back; flags could be missed and corners cut. I have seen a man thrown off his horse by the rider beside him who simply caught him by the foot and lifted it over the saddle. Nobody was hurt and the culprit was disqualified, but his action enabled a horse to win which he had backed to beat his own.

In different places at different times, I've seen a starter so drunk he couldn't sit on his hack, and another who was carried half-way round the course with the runners. And I have seen two grounded riders settling an argument with their fists in the middle of a ploughed field. It was all part of the fun.

When I was about fifteen, I was offered a ride in the maiden race on a three-year-old filly. A flat-sided brown, she looked as if a sharp five furlongs at Phoenix Park would suit her nicely. I had a gallop on her, and discovered that she jumped toes first, without bending her knees. Not at all the thing for a three and a half mile bank course. To my great disappointment, I wasn't allowed to accept the ride – the young man who did was carried in on a stretcher.

I was about nineteen when I first rode in a point to point. The event, inaccurately named the 'Sportsman's Race', was for half-breds and took place at the end of the programme. There were nine competitors of which four finished. One of these was my friend, Joan. I was relieved to see her passing the post as I had grave doubts about her horse, a borrowed brown animal called Shennanigan. Never was a horse less well named. He was a lethargic creature, mainly Irish Draught; he'd a big jump in him, but a big stick was required to get it out, and shennanigans weren't his thing. The start was delayed while a rider topped up with Dutch courage in the bar. He fell off at the first fence.

There was a ladies' allowance of 7lbs, bringing the weights down to twelve stone. I weighed nine stone, Joan about seven. In spite of ordinary saddles and clothes, our leadcloths were so heavy we could hardly lift them. There was a wild stampede for the first fence, then the ploughed ground began to sort the field out. The first big bank brought down three, and the water two more. The rest of us hung on. It seemed a very long way. It was pouring with rain and growing dusk when we finished; it had been raining on and off for weeks. I got a faceful of mud from the leader at the last fence and wasn't sure where the winning post was. My mare Matilda and I were a decent third.

My neighbours were charitable and gave us a great welcome. Mind you, I don't know why anyone was insane enough to back any of us. The whipper-in on his grey horse cleared the course at the finish of each race, galloping up the straight scattering stray children and dogs. As he led us, soaking wet and plastered with mud from head to foot, back to the paddock, I heard a woman say, 'Imagine! The grey horse has all the races won.'

In later years I had mixed success, never winning but being placed twice more. I was generally riding something which was earning its keep in other ways, and none was more than four years old. I was under the impression that our point to point was typical of the sport, and was astonished when I went to visit a cousin who is the long-time master of a pack in the south of England.

It was May, and I was asked to act as fence steward at a local point to point. The course, which would look old-fashioned today, was 'once round' with natural cut-and-laid fences, all so amazingly neat that it might have been a proper steeplechase meeting. Another surprise was the segregation of the sexes. Ladies' races were new to me.

I'd heard of them, of course. I could remember my mother's horror when she realised that her precious teenage daughter was going to compete against a lot of rough men . . . men who might even be heard to utter a naughty word occasionally. Lady riders, she believed, confined themselves to exclaiming 'Drat!' 'Bother!' or, in extreme cases, 'Damn!' I had already been buying and selling horses in fairs for two years at the time, and cattle for longer than that. Besides being immune to oaths, I knew that the age of chivalry was by no means dead and also that there was no chivalry at all among women. Now, about ten years later, I saw them collecting, wearing fur coats over their colours, smoking, talking, very much at ease. 'Darling!' they cried, '*how* are you? Are you *terribly* well?'

The answer to this was, 'Oh, my *dear*, revoltingly so!'

I was asked to stand on a road which the runners had to cross, and make sure that nobody missed a flag. A soft job, I thought, as I drove back to my post in a Land Rover for the fourth time. The next race was the ladies event and I could hear high-pitched abuse two fields away. Two young women, sworn rivals and deadly enemies were approaching at the head of the field.

On the road, which they reached together, the smaller lady's horse ran out and cannoned into the other. Both had to swerve and pull up, while three more runners went on into the lead. Neither said bother, or even damn. Instead, as they wrenched their horses round, they hurled threats and abuse which would have made a bargee blush. They forced their mounts over the hedge from a standstill and galloped away, still screaming at each other. Another rider actually pulled up in order to yell at me, 'Report those bitches or I'll report *you*.' I didn't.

After the races, I dined with the judge and some visiting hunt staff. An MFH asked me, 'Is it true that they have mixed races in Ireland?'

I said that it was.

'But isn't it dangerous?'

I said, 'The women seem to survive.'

'I wasn't talking about the women.'

A white haired man chimed in, 'Wonderful fighters, the

Irish. Think of Gallipoli and Ypres! No troops to touch 'em for courage.'

The MFH wasn't convinced. 'They weren't asked to compete against Miss X and Mrs Y,' he said.

Racing in the Home Counties was disappointing in some ways. The horses were so often worn out 'chasers, nothing with any improvement in it. It seemed to me like a bad imitation of steeplechasing, rather than the nursery for 'chasers that my own country was.

I've said before that racing is addictive. Here to prove it is a story said to be true, about a man who was a landlord in this parish two hundred years ago. There was a little church on his estate, and he swore that if his horse won a certain race he would redecorate the church from top to bottom. The parishioners were delighted when the horse duly won, and the landlord immediately got the decorators in. He had the church painted from steeple to crypt in his racing colours.

For many years I had an annual holiday in England, spending time with people who had bought horses from me. Generally I went in the short gap between hay and harvest – my May trip was for a wedding. Spring was a busy time.

The point to point should have been a warning to lie low, but it wasn't. (I had been reported for failing to report the warring women, as warned.) But no, I was landed with the job of judging in a small show a week later.

Dealers should never be tempted to judge at shows. I was to be asked to do so many times in Ireland, but always refused firmly. The snags range from discouraging canvassers to accidentally giving an award to an animal you have owned briefly and failed to recognise. I have hardly ever heard anyone say a good word for a judge unless, of course, he had been given first prize. Then it is different. The judge is a sound man, discerning and right-minded. Anyone mad enough to judge in his own area could be subjected to abuse and even threats; I have seen and heard it happen. But I thought I would be safe in England. The show was a local affair, the prizes small, the publicity almost nil. I was not, let it be said, the first choice. The lady intended for the job chickened out at the last moment. She said she had tonsilitis. Perhaps she had. I reckon she lost her nerve.

The friends I was staying with didn't consult me. I was no more than twenty and had been dealing in a small way for three years. I heard my host talking on the telephone, but couldn't have guessed that I was the subject.

'. . . Of course she will – she'd love to judge . . . Certainly she's capable; she's a bloodstock breeder from Ireland . . .'

Ireland? I listened more closely. But I didn't breed blood-stock.

'. . . Yes, she's an expert on ponies.' (I hated ponies.) 'I'll ask her, but the answer's definitely yes, she will judge.'

'Who will?' I asked.

'You will.'

Protests were in vain. 'Just a few little ponies – nothing to it,' said my host airily.

The only little thing was the ring, which was more suited to a dog show. I stood quaking in the middle of it, with a scornful ring steward, old enough to be my grandfather, holding a basket of rosettes. All the rest of the space was occupied by a milling throng of ponies. Under 13.2 was the height limit; the smallest could have walked under a dinner table. Some were ridden by weeping tots, others by hard-bitten little girls of twelve or more. I stared at them, horrified. 'Where do I start?' I muttered to the steward. He shrugged his shoulders. 'Walk on,' I said, as firmly as I could.

Some did. One pony grazed its way along, another firmly backed out of the ring. I began to gain a little confidence. There were twenty-three ponies left, and I sorted out about a dozen obvious no-hopers and asked them to leave the ring. That was my first serious mistake.

I got the remainder to walk and trot round in the confined

The sheltered child, in 1935

Bonnetted and gaitered,
with Nanny

Riding Packy

With Batty, the pony we drove during the war
1947 – the car is back on the road

With my father

Saturday's child

Tiger

Sugar Bush, who began by bolting with the hayrake and went on to become an international show jumper

Glenn

With John on our wedding day

Evening feed

In the old orchard (ideal for ewes and lambs) with Ben

With my grandson Jack   (*photo Terry O'Rourke*)

space. Then I removed two that were lame and one which was thinking about kicking the pony behind. Mistake number two.

Judging the remainder was easier. I stood three in front and five behind – there were eight rosettes. The difficulty was to place first and second. They were both greys, very much alike. Nervous of spending too much time, I examined the teeth of each. One was five years old, the other had long yellow fangs, deeply pitted and grooved. I gave first prize to the five-year-old. My limited dealing experience had taught me to place little value on an old horse, however brilliant. I had made my third and most serious mistake.

Outside the ring, I was mobbed by the mothers of the tiny children I had sent out at the beginning. Most of them would have been more at home on rocking-horses. I tried to reason with them – the mothers, not the tots – noticed the steely glint in their eyes, and fled.

Next came the mothers of the no-hopers. How, I was asked, did I expect a child to have a successful showing career if discouraged right from the start? And who was I anyway? And what did they know about ponies in Ireland? And what was this rubbish about bloodstock? And how old was I?

I had never been taught that useful maxim of the Duke of Wellington's: never apologise – never explain. Muttering apologies and explanations, I made it as far as the secretary's tent. There I collapsed into a deck chair which, as in a bad movie, also collapsed, with me folded up inside it. From this position of weakness, I had to ward off the final attack, from the mother of the rider of the old pony.

Didn't I know who she was? Didn't I know the five-year-old had never won anything. Didn't I know what the old pony had won? Didn't I realise it had been supreme champion at the Royal Blankshire?

Here, the secretary made matters worse by saying, 'I doubt if Marjorie would remember as far back as that. It was pre-war.'

The lady's wrath being diverted, I struggled out of the deck chair and escaped.

91

Yes, judges should be elderly, able and thick-skinned. Since then I have successfully avoided judging any animals except the children's pets at a dog show. Even there, the atmosphere was charged with menace.

An old friend of mine, a marvellous judge, was asked to officiate at a lightweight hunter class when he was well over seventy. He rode all but one of the dozen animals presented; a Dales pony, hairy legged and about fifteen hands high. 'Why didn't you judge my horse?' demanded the lady owner afterwards.

'He's in the wrong class. He's a Native Pony, not a hunter.'

'Nonsense. I've hunted him twice a week all season.'

To which the exasperated judge replied, 'Well, what do you expect me to do about that? Burst into tears?' Horse and rider flounced out of the ring. Judging is a job for heroes.

CHAPTER TWELVE

FROM PLACE TO PLACE

Looking back, I'm amazed at how well I used to get about without owning a car. I was twenty-one when I bought my first, a Fiat 'Topolino', and it was anything but reliable. Up till then I relied on bike, train, bus or lifts. Even so, I managed to go to all the big horse fairs.

Even when I'd bought a car, it was another eight or nine years before I got something strong enough to pull a double trailer. I drove my own Morris Minor or a hired mini, and the horse went by rail. Occasionally, I hired a big car and a great ungainly trailer – a Lolode, I think it was called – but only in times of great need.

One such time occurred when I was trying hard to catch up on business after having been laid up for months because of my back injury. It was the end of the year, a time when horsedealers generally manage to rest from making a precarious living. I soldiered on.

Holiday travel means delays for everything from tourists to parcels. A load of horses missing the last boat before Christmas would be held up at the port for a week at least. This almost happened to me. I had three young horses in the stable, eating hay and soaked sugar-beet pulp, waiting for shipment to Yorkshire in January. Suddenly, an SOS arrived from my best customer: 'Send on the horses, and two decent two-year-olds to go with them. I want them before the New Year.'

It was mid December. I made a booking for the Dublin boat, and set off in a freezing fog to buy two youngsters I'd marked down near Killaloe. I had allowed myself two days to buy and bring them home and to despatch all five. At Killaloe, I found that both animals had been sold the day before.

This was serious. I went first to O'Callaghan's Mills where the same buyer had again been ahead of me, then to Ennis, where I found nothing suitable. In Ennis, I heard of a couple of likely horses near Kilrush. The winter's day was drawing in; eating a sandwich as I drove, I headed west. It was late afternoon when I bought a roan gelding from a farmer in Moyasta. I bought the second, a grey, by the light of a street lamp, in Carrigaholt, the last village before Loop Head.

It is at least a hundred miles to Carrigaholt. I went home, hired a car and trailer next day, and drove to Kilkee, where I loaded both horses. About a mile from Bunratty, on the way home, the gearbox seized up. It was getting dark, I was alone, there wasn't a house in sight. The horses stamped and whinnied as the trailer bumped onto the grass verge. Both were unbroken. They were to be put on the train the following afternoon, along with the three at home. I tried to flag down cars without success.

At last a man came along on a bicycle with a bagful of groceries. By good fortune, he was eager to help, and – just as important – he was used to horses. We unloaded them on the busy Shannon road in the dark, and took them to his house. There we crammed them both into the only shed he had – a henhouse. He had no car and it was miles to the nearest garage, so I walked to Bunratty, caught a bus to Limerick, got a lift to Nenagh and another one to within a mile of home. I walked the last bit.

Next day, I borrowed a Land Rover and went to collect my property. I had rung a garage to take in the hired car. I loaded the horses, thanked my kind helper (who refused money), and transferred them to the railway wagon in Nenagh. I hadn't much time to load the others, so quickly hustled the two quietest into the trailer and tried to start the Land Rover. It wasn't having any. With the help, if that's the word, of a man who was terrified of horses and was dying, he said, of the 'flu, I decanted the horses, transferred the trailer to the tractor and loaded up again. I also phoned for a car to meet me in the station to speed up the collection of the last horse.

The tractor had no cab and its top speed was twelve miles an hour. I arrived at the station frozen, put the horses in the wagon and drove the hired car home for the last one. There I found a message had just arrived, saying that all shipping from the North Wall was stopped for two weeks.

As I returned four horses to their stables, I reflected bitterly that I had overspent on the last two, which had probably missed their job; that the car was in a garage thirty miles away; that it and the borrowed Land Rover would have to be repaired and paid for; and that I was almost certainly about to come down with 'flu.

It could have been worse. If the telephone call had been half an hour later, I'd have had either another big transport bill to pay, or five horses stranded at the port. Shipping agents' fees, food and stabling would have more than used up the profit.

Early in the New Year, I sent the five horses to the boat by lorry. My troubles were over for a while but my customer's were only beginning. He went to meet the boat at Birkenhead, where he discovered it had been diverted to Holyhead. So he had to drive across Wales in a blizzard and broke down on Snowdon. . . .

I often grumbled about inadequate transport, but many people carried on thriving businesses or ran successful farms without a car. They depended on lifts, and it was normal for those who had cars to fill them with people who hadn't. I learned early that it was inadvisable to give lifts to farmers on the way home from fairs, as they were usually half jarred. Today, a woman on her own would be worried about mugging or even rape; then one's only difficulty was to dislodge the passenger from the car without actually taking him home. But it's hard to leave an elderly man on the side of the road on a chilly winter's day, even if he does seem to be somewhat under the weather.

I was heading home after a long and unprofitable day at Newmarket fair in North Cork. 'Are you going far?' I asked.

'That depends on yourself.' My passenger lit a large and smelly pipe. 'I'll travel as far as I'm carried. I like to travel.' His tone was aggressive. I shut up.

After a time, I remarked, 'There were some beautiful foals at Newmarket today.'

The man turned his head and glared at me through a cloud of smoke. 'Horses aren't beautiful,' he said at last. 'If you think they are, you have no eye for beauty.' He puffed at his pipe for a bit and then said, 'But then, not many has the true eye.'

'You have it, I suppose,' I said sarcastically.

'Oh aye. I have it all right.' He smoked in silence for a minute or two. 'What beauty,' he demanded suddenly, 'is there in skin and flesh and blood and bones? Horses! Women! They can change any time. Do you dare to deny it?' I didn't dare.

I was driving into Charleville as he spoke, and offered to set him down there. 'No, there's men in Charleville that don't like me. Take me to Limerick.' Hoping that the men of Limerick would be more tolerant, I drove on.

I thought he'd gone to sleep – the pipe had gone out and his chin was on his chest. But suddenly he startled me by shouting, 'Stop here.' We were on an open road, not far from Croom. A stark white bungalow stood at the roadside, surrounded by spiked railings. It was so new that the grass hadn't grown over the builder's rubble. The railings were painted cobalt blue with silver spikes.

My passenger sat up and pointed with his pipe. 'Talk about beauty,' he cried, 'that's the real apple. If you have an eye for beauty like me, you can't be happy under thatch. It's in slates and cement and good hard-wearing paint that you see it.'

'Is this where you live? Will I put you down here?'

'Oh, you're in a big hurry to get rid of me. If you listen to me, my dear woman, you might learn something.'

I managed not to suggest that he might learn some manners, and set him down thankfully just outside Limerick at a pub (slated, and painted emerald green picked out in pink).

I steadfastly refused lifts for weeks afterwards.

Years later, when I was as much interested in buying a good sheepdog as a good horse, I was driving with my husband along a mountain road. We were heading for a farm where, we had heard, there was a useful young dog for sale. The day was unpleasant as only a December afternoon can be in the mountains. There was sleet in the rain and a promise of snow to come. There were no houses, no signposts, no villages. We were lost.

When we overtook an old man plodding along with a bundle on his back, we hailed him with all the enthusiasm of Good King Wenceslas. We asked him the way to Jim Daly's house (not his real name), and he answered, 'Aren't I going there myself?'

Had we but known it, the question was rhetorical and the answer was, 'No.'

Delighted, I opened the door and helped him to stow his bundle on the back seat. 'A few little things people gave me for the Christmas,' said the old man, who told us his name was Jerry. 'The times are gone to hell, but most give me a tin of biscuits or a few fags,' he added.

As we drove along, Jerry entertained us with anecdotes, mostly scandalous, and pointed out places where people had been killed. 'Is it much further?' John asked.

'It isn't. You can stop here, at this farm.'

We stopped, and Jerry hurried into the house. Thinking he must have business with Jim Daly, we waited . . . and waited. At last, I went to the door and saw three or four people sitting in front of the fire, drinking. 'Come on in, the two of you and have a jar,' Jerry invited largely. We inquired which was Jim Daly.

'This isn't Daly's at all,' said Jerry. 'I made a mistake. Sit down and take a drink when it's offered you. Isn't it going on Christmas?'

We accepted hot whiskey and lemonade – heavy on whiskey, light on lemonade – but refused to wait for more. Back in the car, we again asked Jerry to tell us the way to Jim Daly's. 'What hurry is on you?' he replied. 'Sure we'll be a long time dead.' A mile or so further on, we reached a house where Jerry said he had to call 'for a minute'. We waited ten minutes, then blew the horn. Jerry appeared, wiping his mouth. 'Take it easy, will you,' he said. 'You couldn't get away from that woman, she's the biggest gabber from hell to Bedlam.'

'If you won't take us to Jim Daly's, you can get out and walk,' I said.

'Walk? Where's your Christian charity, missis? And I near eighty years of age and the season that's in it. Stop here at this cottage.'

'Is it Daly's?'

'It is not, but the woman of the house buried her husband lately. We'll get a few drinks if we play our cards right.' We let him out of the car, telling him to get his few drinks and a lift home while he was at it.

I'd spotted a village in the distance, and there we asked our way. We were wrong by ten miles and had to go back the way we had come, arriving at Jim Daly's as the light faded. It dawned on us that Daly's was the last farm we'd passed before we overtook Jerry, and furthermore, that Jerry had recently left the Daly farm well warmed with Christmas cheer.

It was, of course, a wasted journey, as you can't watch a dog working sheep in the dusk. He looked a nice sort and we agreed to return. Jim invited us in for a cup of tea. 'I'd offer you whiskey,' he said, 'but Jerry emptied the bottle on me – he makes his rounds every year. He'll be legless by now, but he finds his way home like a cat.'

It was cosy in the kitchen but outside the rain streamed down harder than ever. The couple from the next farm arrived and fresh tea was brewed. We agreed that it was a terrible night for an old man to be out walking, and that we must look out for Jerry on the way home. He might have passed out on the side of the road.

He hadn't. When we left, we found him asleep in the back of our car. Woken up by John, none too gently, he had no difficulty in directing us to his own house, which was another five miles out of our way.

Some time after this, we got a late night call from a farmer we knew well who was stranded in the village of Hollyford with a pick-up full of calves and a broken axle. We were happy to help, as this man had helped us when we'd been stranded in the middle of nowhere ourselves. Hollyford is twenty miles away on a mountainous road, and it was 11 p.m. when we reached it.

'It's not just a matter of getting the calves home,' said our friend. 'I can leave them till tomorrow. But I've an old man in the pick-up who asked for a lift this morning.

He's been cadging drinks all day, now he's paralytic and I don't know where he lives.' I wasn't greatly surprised when I looked through the window and saw Jerry, sleeping like a baby.

'I know exactly where he lives,' I said. 'It's not on your road home, or ours.' We transferred the old man to our car and took first him, then the farmer home. Jerry didn't wake when we hauled him out of the pick-up and into the car. In fact he never stirred until we reached his home. I was in the back with him, the two men in the front. 'Wake up, Jerry,' I said. 'You're home.'

Jerry sat up and yawned. He didn't seem particularly surprised to find himself in a different car with a different driver. He climbed out of the car, staggered a little, then turned and shook my hand. 'You know, missis, I like you,' he said. 'Give me a shout the next time you're travelling and I'll come along for the spin.'

CHAPTER THIRTEEN

WEATHER AND CLOCKS

Over the years, I have had many dealings with European buyers of both horses and dogs. Most of them spoke English at least as good as mine, but I have sometimes had to try to deal in my frightful French. Now if it's hard to make small talk in a language you are bad at it's the very devil to try to make money in it. None of the phrase books tell you how to say, 'The bay gelding you bid me for has pulled his stifle,' or 'I mated the smaller bitch with Casey's good doubles dog, but she didn't hold.'

In the end, I gave up and just translated everything literally, using a dictionary. The results reduced my French, Belgian and Swiss customers to fits of laughter, but they got the gist. My school dictionary was too coy to give a word for in season.

'*Elle est en saison*,' I said. '*Pardon?*' '*Elle est sur* – oh God, what's heat? *Elle est chaud. Elle veut s'encoupler.*' '*Pardon?*'

Dutch people seem to speak excellent English, but one of them who arrived here wanting to hire a horse for a day's hunting was the exception that proves the rule, so we conversed in sign language. Like me, he had a phrase book; like mine, it wasn't helpful. We didn't as a rule hire out horses, but as he couldn't get one elsewhere, offered him a plain little chestnut which had been the 'blender' in a bunch of three. Too small for a trooper, he was quiet if little else. The Dutchman searched his phrasebook and summed him up with masterly understatement: 'I think,' he said, 'he will not make history.'

For the next day's hunting, this gentleman acquired a hireling from someone else; a brown animal, known to some of us as 'Scrubbing Brush'. This horse had a rooted objection to jumping. The Dutchman, a good horseman, set him at a low, solid rail. Scrubbing Brush galloped at it, stopped dead, did a vertical take-off, cracked the rail with his heels and dropped like a brick, landing heavily on all four feet. As his unfortunate rider was flung into the air, then deposited violently on the front of the saddle, he yelled, 'Gerr . . . bloot . . . boogaire!'

'You know,' said my husband to me, 'I believe I could learn Dutch.'

I forget if it was this Dutchman or another who said, in careful phrases, 'Ireland is beautiful, but you have no sun and no clocks.' Though I denied this with some force, he did have a point.

Weather is, I suppose, the greatest enemy of the farmer, and in Ireland bad weather means rain. We don't, thank God, get snowed up; we do get bogged down.

There is, of course, a well-worn fallacy about Ireland, namely that it is full of bogs. This is untrue, as is the other fallacy – that the bog idea is nonsense. I live on limestone land which drains overnight. Only five miles away there is a string of bogs reaching away into the midlands.

Bogs don't just sit there; they move about. Their movement is hardly perceptible until a roadway collapses or a building suddenly subsides. I remember asking a farmer if it was safe to cross a certain bog on a horse. He said he thought not. 'Two calves drowned just there,' he said, pointing. 'The roars of them was unmerciful.'

'Here?' I asked, mystified.

'Yes. Just there, where you're standing.' This happened to be on the main Cloughjordan road, some way from the dangerous area. Further questioning established that the calves had met their end some fifty years earlier. The bog had moved about twenty yards in the interval.

This place, Lofty Bog, is one of a chain of three, divided by lanes and roads. 'Lofty' is a popular site for seagulls which wish to nest undisturbed. It is also a burial ground for dead cars and tractors. One day, as I was riding towards a pub called Luckybags, I noticed that a piece of rusty machinery had been dumped at the edge of the bog. It was some sort of antique compressor and was at least six feet square. As I passed, there was a gulping noise and bubbles of marsh gas broke the surface all round the machine, which lurched and settled a few inches. I was visiting friends for the day. When I returned in the evening the bog had swallowed the compressor completely. Nasty.

About fifty yards from the compressor's grave, a small piece of soundish land was used as a site for a dance hall. Funds were restricted and the land was, rightly, cheap. Known as the 'Floating Ballroom', it had a maple floor and a tin roof. When it rained, the noise drowned the band. It had only been used a few times when water began to seep, then to gush through the cracks in the floor; it was soon abandoned.

Part of the bog was traversed by a causeway wide enough for a donkey and cart, and perfectly safe if you took it quietly. Out hunting, we used to gallop along it, feeling the surface shift from side to side and sometimes heave up and down. This was as unnerving for horses as for their riders, and the keenest would slow up, bewildered. Once, a horse and rider ahead of me suddenly tumbled over sideways for no reason that I could see. 'The road went from under me,' said the rider. He was more or less correct.

Those who imagine that Ireland is just one great swamp, often seem to think that bogs are a feature of no other country. I thought so myself until I met a Yorkshire horse dealer (admittedly he was drunk), who argued at great length about the superiority of Yorkshire bogs over the Tipperary variety. He said they were bigger, deeper and wetter, and seemed proud of the fact. 'And the rain is wetter in Ireland,' he said.

'Rubbish. How could it be?'

'It's a well known fact. The drops are closer together.'

Bogs are now things to be explored, written about and protected. They have acquired a certain cachet. I got sidetracked on to bogs, when it was my intention to write about mud. There is nothing good to be said about mud, and nothing to beat the misery of it. Rain, sleet and snow cease to fall eventually. Mud is still around when the rain has stopped. In a farmyard after snow, one encounters the worst kind of all; mud evenly mixed with slush and manure.

One of the things which makes me prefer sheep to cows is that they are so much cleaner. The farmyard used to be dominated by a vast manure heap. Nowadays there are slurry tanks which are at least underground, but it's advisable to shut the windows when they are being emptied.

In the early days of one of the farm organisations, some sensitive souls decided that the word 'dung' should be banned. Instead, farmers were asked to call this substance FYM (farmyard manure), pronounced 'fim'. I never heard anyone do this. People not born to farming often develop an uncanny interest in its nastier aspects, which seems strange to one who is crafty at avoiding them. One 'new-catched' farmer, as my husband used to call them, cordially invited us to go with him to a slurry-handling demonstration and was quite put out when we refused.

Thinking back to the years when I never missed a horse fair, I am almost glad those days have gone. If you have orders for horses, then horses you must buy, come hell or high water. Today you can buy in cushioned comfort at Kill, if that's your line, and all sales are under cover. There was no comfort at the fairs, which took place regardless of the weather.

Three years in a row Cahirmee fair in July was almost washed out. I know; I bought twelve horses at those three watery events and spent around ten hours in wet clothes at each. I galloped horses for their wind in paddocks where they sank almost to their knees. In fact, it was possible to *trot* them for their wind – a couple of rounds had them blowing hard enough for any weakness to be obvious.

At one of these fairs I was caught in a thunderstorm which left me so drenched I couldn't possibly go to a café for a meal. Most of the shops in the little town were shut, but one, specialising in menswear, had a notice up: CLOSING DOWN SALE. EVERYTHING MUST GO. There I bought a shirt and a pair of jeans.

As I needed to put them on, I asked if there was a changing room. The assistant looked doubtful, but showed me upstairs and indicated a dark, cluttered room, where I could see little besides a bed and some stacks of cardboard boxes. There was a bathtowel hanging over a chair, so I undressed and towelled myself dry. Then I put on the new clothes and sat on the side of the bed to lace my shoes. A polite voice beside me said, 'Good evening, miss.' There was an old man in the bed. Since then, I have examined all changing rooms carefully.

On cold days, buyers on their way home from Kilrush fair congregated at Fanny O'Dea's at Lissycasey to be restored by Fanny's famous egg-flips, laced with brandy. I generally pretended to be teetotal when dealing – it was easy then to keep out of pubs. Pubs on fair days were places to be avoided, but I made an exception of Fanny O'Dea's.

105

I suppose we've grown soft. Nothing the weather could do would deter my parents from driving five miles to church or the shops in the gig. Flood water almost to the shafts was a yearly hazard until our by-road was raised by six feet. Cyclists used to go round by the fields.

I remember one truly appalling day with floods of rain and a force ten gale, when my parents were obliged to attend a funeral six miles away. I was taken along to hold the pony while the adults were at the graveside. There was no water-proof footgear other than gumboots to be had, and I can still see my mother standing on one leg emptying the water out of her shoes – with little complaint. Living through this period makes me feel for the coachmen of olden days, perched up on their box seats in all weathers. No wonder so many of them took to the bottle.

Now that I seldom need to sit for hours in wet clothes or suffer the pain of chilblains, I sometimes wonder if there is much to be said for the Spartan life. Does it benefit any-body? And if so, why is it so bad for animals? Cold is less of an enemy than rain and wind. Shelter is the first requisite for animals in the winter. If they feel cold they eat more to keep their energy up, and are subject to infections and lung disorders. This applies to cattle, sheep and horses, so why not to grooms and shepherds too? Stuffy stables and low crowded buildings are almost as bad but not quite. I have never known animals which had shelter and space to breathe come to much harm.

Sheep in particular are good weather prophets. They hate the wet and start moving to a sheltered part of the field well before the rain arrives. They lie down when it's going to rain as cattle do. Having eaten well while the grass was dry, they lie down to digest the meal. Then they move to the dryest place they can find.

Of course, our foxhunting Dutchman, like many others, only encountered Irish weather in the depths of winter, so his opinions were biased. But what of his other statement, that we have no clocks? We have clocks; we just don't consult them very often.

I was trained in punctuality from an early age by my ex-army father, and such habits stick. I still keep time myself, but don't expect my countrymen to do likewise. It's a mistake to think that Irish people get pleasure from being late; we are, as a race, indifferent to the passage of time. This must surely reduce the incidence of stress-related diseases. 'The man who made time made lots of it' is an oft repeated proverb.

One true story sums up what I am trying to say neatly. An Englishman, a lorry-driver, had moved to Ireland and was looking for a job. He applied to the owner of a haulage business, and made an appointment to meet him at his home at 8 a.m. the following morning. At eight o'clock sharp, he was ringing the haulier's doorbell. Then he decided the bell wasn't working and thumped the knocker. After a time, a window above his head opened, and a lady in her nightdress looked out. 'What the hell do you want?'

'I want to see the boss. I have an appointment for eight o'clock.'

The haulier's wife consulted her watch. 'Why, it's only eight o'clock now!' she exclaimed, and left the sadder and wiser Englishman to wait in his car until a more Christian hour.

CHAPTER FOURTEEN

A CHANGE OF DIRECTION

I was in my thirties by the time making a living ceased to be a non-stop punishing struggle. So it was for all farmers in Ireland in the 'fifties and 'sixties – I certainly wasn't alone. My horses saved me from disaster again and again, although the bank manager found this impossible to believe, even when confronted with figures.

Farming was so bad that any spare money was usually spent on the only paying proposition – the cows. I could have borrowed to buy more cows, but not to fill my horse contracts. Everywhere I went buying, the cows were fat, the horses thin. I bought a miserably thin brown colt which was drawing milk to the creamery; a narrow, high-withered creature which looked less than his height.

The Milkman, as I named him, was a lot too sharp for the two elderly brothers who owned him. One would lead him nervously by the bridle, while the other clung to the milk cans, saying, 'Whoa blood! Whoa the wild one!' in soothing tones. They were pleased to sell the thin youngster and bought an elderly heavy mare. This one went stone blind, but continued to draw the milk-cart, regardless.

I collected the Milkman from the farm, and complimented the brothers pointedly on a lovely green field, on which he had certainly not been grazing. 'Ah, that field would fatten a bicycle,' said one brother. 'No, that wouldn't be possible,' said the other, more down to earth.

Generally, my countrymen aren't lacking in imagination. I have been warned to mind the telegraph wires when I was jumping a horse I meant to buy, which suggested a leap of ten feet or so. But a truly literal mind sometimes occurs. I bought an emaciated colt which I called Castaway, and discovered that he was infested with lice. I was shaking louse powder over him from a canister when a customer arrived in the yard. He watched me through a cloud of DDT for a few minutes, then asked me what I was doing. Thinking that a silly question deserved a silly answer, I said 'I'm shaking fertiliser on him to make him grow.'

'You're wasting your time,' said the buyer, 'It couldn't possibly work.'

Poor Castaway was one of the thinnest horses I've ever seen. I bought him cheaply, the 'sweetener' in a bunch of four. I was lucky, as he soon filled out on good grass (the bicycle-fattening variety) and went to the Metropolitan Police.

In the dreadful winter of 1962–63 even well-off people had a job to keep condition on their animals. Hay wasn't merely dear, it was unobtainable. Oats couldn't be bought except at a crazy price. Under-nourished foals and yearlings began to appear in the cattle fairs, brought from the West by lorry.

I bought a grey yearling, rising two, for £25, hardly knowing if he was a horse or a pony in the making. He was named

Hungry Hill after the place of his birth in the Arra Mountains. The old man I bought him from took the money and went to ground in the nearest pub, but I winkled him out and he agreed to lead the colt home. Hours passed and he hadn't arrived. I set out on a bike to look for him. Rounding a corner, about a mile from home, I met the old man, plodding along, halter rope in hand. It was a long rope, and the halter was trailing along the road at the end of it. There was no sign of Hungry Hill, and I found him nibbling briars a long way back. As for the old man, having found the horse, it seemed I'd lost the seller. However, as I passed the Thatched Cottage Inn I noticed a halter lying outside. A rope attached to it led under the door into the Select Bar.

That winter, some non-horsy friends of mine took pity on a tinkers' pony and bought it for their little boy. It was quiet to ride, but even when the grass came it was thin and weak. They asked me to have a look at it. I did. It was a miserable little dun, its mane and tail clipped right off, apparently with a blunt knife. Its tiny feet made me wonder, and I examined its teeth. I'd been told it was five years old, but no, it was a yearling. It was also an entire colt. These facts came as a shock to the owners, who optimistically went in search of the tinker they had bought it from. They searched in vain – which was just as well, since the pony grew into a cob, keeping pace with the growth of his child rider for years.

At last the tide turned, I began to relax. I was able to afford to reclaim all the low-lying part of the farm and to stock it with cattle; I bought a new car, upped the turnover of horses, replaced the tractor and took two weeks holiday in England every summer. I got commissions to buy police horses and troopers in half dozens rather than singly, I bought hunters for private customers as well as unbroken stock and potential show jumpers.

When coaching marathons became popular, I got orders

111

for matched pairs, usually of Irish Draught type or, much more difficult, requests to buy something to match a horse in a poor quality colour snapshot.

Suddenly there was a craze for having everything matching: I think Laura Ashley may have had something to do with it. As rooms blossomed with matching chintzes on every piece of furniture with the motif repeated on the wallpaper, the fashion spread to co-ordinated dressing and – for those who were interested – to matched pairs, or teams, of horses. Those who couldn't afford such things contented themselves with buying spotted, odd-coloured, or in any way eye-catching mounts.

The horse world is full of old proverbs, many of which are nonsense. One of these is, 'A good horse is never a bad colour.' The saying probably referred originally to piebalds, skewbalds and Appaloosas, which are now highly prized. Any of these is preferable to a washy colour, although owners have ways of getting round washiness. Washy chestnuts are described as 'Palamino' and washy browns as 'dark dun' when they are for sale.

In my long association with horses, I have learned to connect certain colours with characteristics. A washy colour may go with a wimpish temperament, and a bright colour with an excitable nature. As for markings, we all know the old rhyme about white socks:

> One – buy him,
> Two – try him,
> Three – suspect him,
> Four – reject him.

Another version turns this one upside down:

> One white sock, keep him not a day,
> Two white socks, send him far away,
> Three white socks, sell him to a friend,
> Four white socks, keep him to the end.

When horses were more plentiful, it was difficult to sell one with white 'stockings' above the knee. I knew a man – I'll call him Tom – who owned a chestnut, a big handsome gelding, with one foreleg white almost to the elbow. The horse was to be sold at a fair, and Tom bought a bottle of hair dye in a shade called 'Autumn Glow'. The colour, as shown on the packet, exactly matched the horse.

Tom went to a lot of trouble. He bandaged the fetlock down to the hoof so as to leave a convincing 'sock' and soaked the rest in dye. It dried out a cruel shade of egg-yolk yellow. Tom applied more dye and the leg turned bright orange with a faint tinge of green; whereupon he thought better of it, and tried to wash the dye out. 'Up to six shampoos,' said the instructions. About eight shampoos later the leg was back to the egg-yolk colour. At that stage, I bought the horse myself and turned him out to fade. Months later, the leg was still yellowish, but he was a good horse and made money. He won working hunter classes under the name 'Autumn Glow'.

The prejudice against chestnuts, especially mares, is deep-rooted, although it is the second commonest colour after bay. It is also dominant, chestnut parents being obliged to produce chestnut foals, whether they want to or not.

I have owned scores of chestnut mares, including two absolute devils. Why they didn't kill me between them I shall never know. I have also owned dozens which were as quiet as wood. This phrase 'as quiet as wood', reminds me of a less apt metaphor, 'as quiet as a lamb'. A quiet lamb is probably ill.

A dealer I know has another simile, 'As gentle as a bee'. After my experience with Paul and the hayrake, this sounds to me like a joke in poor taste.

There is an old Irish saying, 'A black horse with sorra a white hair will kill seven men.' I have found this, if not literally true, to have some foundation. I have never known a horse that was black all over which didn't have a flawed character.

113

Sulkiness is often the problem rather than real badness. Black is not a popular colour (outside the Household Cavalry) nor yet a usual one. Yet the equine heroes of fiction are frequently black or – equally uncommon – white. Black Beauty and Black Bess are obvious examples of the first, while damsels in distress were rescued by knights riding white stallions – not chestnut mares.

I wouldn't buy a piebald for myself, but a certain lady had a fancy for one and offered a fancy price to match. She wasn't worried about performance, only colour and reasonable looks. Accordingly, I bought a pretty piebald mare, only to find that my customer had changed her mind.

The mare, like the lady, had a temperament. She looked attractive (the mare, I mean) and had two paces, a walk and a slowish gallop. She didn't believe in jumping and was slow in the uptake except when crossing a muddy gap. Then, she would drop as if shot and roll. Most coloured horses have pony blood, and rolling in gateways is a pony's trick. In the case of a piebald or skewbald, there may be a protective instinct to camouflage the white patches. I have found light greys far dirtier in their stables than bays or browns – they need too much grooming for my taste.

Some horses keep themselves scrupulously clean; others do not. I will refrain from further human comparisons.

The dirtiest horse I ever owned was Lily. This oddly named mare was cream coloured and had to be washed all over every time she was ridden. In addition to normal ways of getting filthy, she would wriggle out of her rugs and lie down in the wettest places she could find.

When I sold her, Lily was renamed Cornflakes. They say it's unlucky to change a horse's name, which was the reason I hadn't done so. Lily/Cornflakes brought no luck to anybody.

One of the pleasanter aspects of dealing in the 'sixties was that it was then that the meat trade began to fall off. No longer was a three-year-old's value reckoned by what he weighed. No longer were good Irish Draught mares sent to the factory the first time that they missed being in foal. Right up to the early 'seventies, when prices rose steeply, a smallish, unbroken filly was worth more for the meat trade than anything else.

In earlier times, I had bought many a horse which would otherwise never have had a chance to prove his worth. Some dealers bought only animals which had been salvaged from lorry loads of 'killers', getting an even number of bargains and duds. I remember seeing a nice little horse about 15.1 hands being led on to a shipper's lorry at Cahirmee fair. I was suspicious because he had been clipped out, and let him go. Another, less cynical, customer liked him and gave profit – he was still costing only £60. The lorry departed, and the buyer told everybody about his bargain. Another customer got interested, said he might give profit. They took the horse into the barrack field to canter him, and he dropped dead almost at once. The boastful buyer was left with nothing but a body to dispose of.

I have bought a few off the lorries myself, usually unbroken Irish Draught types with size, suitable for police work. One of my favourites was also one of my first bargains – Mona by name.

I was in Nenagh, buying cattle in the square, when I saw a sad looking bunch of horses being loaded for the boat. I knew the dealer who had bought them locally, and he invited me to 'Pick where you like for £35.' On closer inspection, they weren't a brilliant lot, but I sorted out a nice type of five year old grey mare, about 15.3 hands.

Mona was well made and not common; only one feature hinted at humble origins. On her upper lip, she wore a small white moustache which grew sideways from a centre parting. I hastily clipped it off. Mona had been broken and gone in harness. She had a perfect mouth, a lovely nature and was as sound as a bell. Even my mother enjoyed riding her.

I sold Mona for double her cost and still cheap to a dealer

from Yorkshire. He passed her on to Rowley Harker, for many years master of the Jedforest Hunt. The dealer reported this sale on the phone to a friend. As he was sparing with his aitches, dealer number two thought he'd said, 'Marjorie's grey mare's gone to Rollearca.' So he rang me up and told me that Mona had been retired to stud and covered by a son of Nearco. That's how rumours start – not that I believed him. Years later, Rowley Harker sent me a photograph of himself and Mona, saying he'd hunted hounds off her for many seasons and wanted another. 'Preferably clean shaven,' he added.

Another horse of mine which was lucky to survive, was my only purchase at Goff's Bloodstock Sales. A dark bay thoroughbred filly, she looked like the makings of a show pony. She cost fifty-five guineas, and the underbidder was a dogfood man.

Piccolina hadn't the temperament for showing, being a wild, scatterbrained creature. She also grew too big, which meant she was the dealers' nightmare, an undersized misfit – and a misfit with a cold back, at that. I sold this one after six strenuous months. She was more or less rideable, and might have made a polo pony had she been less nervous. Unfortunately, she wasn't up to the weight of anyone strong enough to control her. I sold her for £85 (a huge loss in real terms) and didn't expect to hear anything good about her. Wrong again. Piccolina found her true vocation in life and won fourteen pony races at Northholt Park.

Not long after I sold Piccolina, horses changed my life. I was lying in bed with a bad go of 'flu, when a friend of mine called, saying he wanted to borrow one of my horses for an Englishman to go hunting on. 'He can borrow one from somebody else,' I said fretfully. 'Why should I lend my horse to some ham-fisted tourist? Is he any good on a horse?'

'Good? Of course he is. Johnny Quarton goes like a pigeon across country. No nerves at all – nice fellow too.'

'I don't care how nice he is. He's not getting one of my young horses – he'd knock it up.'

'But I told him you'd lend him Vicky. I could bring him up to see you if you like.'

'I don't like, and you shouldn't have told him anything of the kind. Do go away – I'm dying.'

The Englishman borrowed from somebody more charitable, and I missed meeting my future husband. It was years before he returned to Ireland.

Around the time when I refused to lend John Quarton a horse, a field adjoining my farm was let to an elderly farmer who kept a dozen bullocks in it. This was a nuisance, as the field was landlocked, and I had to let him drive his cattle across my land. (Eventually, I bought the field myself.) The farmer, Mick Doheny, owned a black-brown mare which he turned in to the field to fatten her up. He reckoned she would fetch £60 for beef.

The mare might have fattened faster if she hadn't persisted in jumping the boundary fence and joining my horses. It seemed a pity to allow such a good natural jumper to go for beef, so I bought her for £60. I tried to sell her to the Household Cavalry, but she wasn't black enough. Then, as no other customers turned up, I passed her on for £80 to a Yorkshire dealer who sold her to John Quarton, who hunted with the Middleton and the Sinnington Hounds in Yorkshire.

John hunted the mare, which was called Amazon, and she was a brilliant performer. At the end of the season, he sold her to the field master, Sir William Brooksbank, for £350.

Money for old rope, thought John, and asked the dealer to buy him another horse from the same farm. I got a phone call from the dealer who'd bought Amazon, not saying who his customer was, just that he wanted a decent three-year-old gelding and had a preference for a grey.

I went to the next fair, which was at Thurles, and soon

117

spotted what looked like a suitable horse. I feared, though, that he might be expensive, because he was as beautifully turned out as if he'd been going to a show. He wore a bridle with gleaming brass buckles, no saddle, and was being led about by a monk in habit and sandals.

I was a bit shy of doing business with a monk, although I knew that his monastery, Mount St Joseph Abbey in Roscrea, was famous for its livestock and garden produce. The monk was called Brother Lazarian, and it was next to impossible to deal with him because he had been told the least he could take and it was too much for me. 'I trained the colt myself – he has a great mouth,' he said, and with that he kilted up his habit and vaulted on to the grey's bare back. He trotted up and down the street and offered to take the horse over jumps if I could find any. It was no good; we both had a price limit. However I agreed to go to the Monastery and haggle with Brother Lazarian's superior.

I did this, driving up to the main door which stood open and walking in. At once, a group of monks rushed at me and drove me out with shooing movements, shutting the doors, which they leaned against as if I might attempt to force my way in. 'No women allowed in here,' one of them gasped in a tone of horror. Feeing guilty and ashamed, I allowed myself to be led away to the farmyard.

I was still unable to give the monks' price, and they sold the grey elsewhere. Then my dealer upped his price and I was able to give the new owner a bit of profit and get some myself. John got the horse and he was almost as lucky as the mare, Amazon.

After this, John fell out with our go-between and came to Ireland to do his own horsetrading. Not long afterwards, he decided to stay. 'If you can't beat 'em, join 'em,' he said. If Amazon had found her way to some French dinner table, my life would have been very different.

Marriage had not been high on my list of priorities. I was undomesticated and unmaternal to a degree. I was indeed fortunate in getting not only a wonderful husband, but a readymade family of seven as well. I produced one daughter of my own with reasonable efficiency, and adapted to a new lifestyle with ease.

Women move house more often than not when they marry, but I was fortunate. It was John who left home and moved to Ireland. From the moment he arrived, it seemed as if he'd always lived here. Impossible to imagine Crannagh without him.

My wedding day sticks in my mind for other reasons besides the conventional ones. I refused, much to my mother's annoyance, to wear white or have a bevy of bridesmaids. I compromised by going to a hairdresser for the first time in my life. As I also took the milk to the Creamery and the service was at eleven a.m., good timing was needed. As I drove to Nenagh at sixty miles an hour, a cow wandered out of a gateway on to the road. Forced to drive *behind* her (in front would have been fatal for both of us), I just grazed her backside with my wing mirror as she suddenly decided to go back. The other wing mirror touched the nose of another cow following behind. No harm done, but I arrived at the Creamery suffering from more than wedding nerves.

Later, duly curled and waved, I waited on my cousin's arm to walk up the aisle. I was to do this to the strains of the hymn 'Lead us, Heavenly Father, lead us.' My cousin, another John, knowing my general vagueness, and not at all surprised when I was late, hissed at me, 'When the choir gets to the words, "keenest woe", we go in. Left, right ... keep in step with me.' Almost overcome with a fit of the giggles, I did as I was told.

I carried on with horsedealing almost without a break. I don't recommend buying a bunch of troopers in a busy fair when seven months pregnant, nor yet trying to carry on all business from the car because the baby's in a carry cot in the back, but both can be and were done. We were immensely happy.

From then on, the horsedealing remained mainly my concern, as did the buying and selling of cattle. John turned to tillage and sheep, and, the only interest we didn't already share, Border Collie dogs.

CHAPTER FIFTEEN

SHEEP ON THE CHEAP

When John and I were married, the recession in farming was coming to an end. Everybody was being encouraged to take out huge loans and to 'think big'. What a contrast to the running battle I had carried on with the bank for so many years! The immediate result was that some farmers did indeed think big and, with the help of massive cash injections, progressed from being small farmers to being large, or even enormous farmers. Many thought too big, and went out of business.

Naturally, our horsedealing business depended on loans, but only those we knew we could meet. Neither of us had ever been in a position to avail ourselves of the sort of aid being offered, so we did without. Luckily for us, as a sudden leap in interest rates did for a lot of people.

Being confined to the house more than I was used to, as I couldn't expect John to take to the perpetual picnic which my life had been for years, I wanted a small enterprise to carry out on my own. I bought thirty in-lamb ewes. Thinking small, you see. Now the popular idea of a small farmer has changed surprisingly little with the passing of time. He may be shown as a carefree character, strolling about among his livestock and presumably living on fresh air and spring water. The other popular image is of an embittered slave, trudging through the slurry in leaky gumboots; working eighteen hours a day, seven days a week in order to survive. Equally untrue.

My sheep were a viable enterprise as long as they were housed. As soon as they went out to grass I had problems. John had a good dog by then, and offered to lend him, but the ewes were my thing – I refused. Even a modest farming operation is viable if carried out by one person. As soon as you reach a point where you have to pay for help, there is such a huge jump in expenditure that you have to buy more stock. Which means borrowing, which is where we came in.

'If you won't work Roy, you'd better have a dog of your own,' said John. He pointed out that a dog is on call day or night, all the year round. It doesn't appreciate a holiday, but is eager to get back to its work and will go until it drops. This is not normally the outlook of a human helper – indeed it shouldn't be. There is no need to live a dog's life unless you are a dog.

I said firmly that I could manage. I couldn't, of course. The sheep were a wild bunch, and I couldn't get near enough to them to count them. I couldn't round them up – the field was large. I did my herding from the back of a horse, as today some use motorbikes. The snag about either horse or bike is that while you are opening a gate for the flock, they will have quickly hurried back to where they came from. While you are shutting the gate, having fetched them again, they may go anywhere. One thing they won't do is wait quietly in a bunch.

'I'll teach them to follow a tin of nuts,' I said. They didn't need teaching. I was sometimes in danger of being trampled under foot with my tin of nuts. Wherever I went, there was an eager, bleating, barging crowd at my heels; I couldn't get away from the brutes.

The reason why I was so reluctant to use a dog was that John was an outstanding sheepdog handler, and I felt intimidated by his professional approach. He would stand at a gate, sometimes shouting, sometimes whistling and his dog or dogs would race down the field, gather every sheep, fetch, drive or pen them without missing a trick. I was afraid of spoiling the dog and of making a fool of myself. I read books on sheep management instead. One of these books gave a list of necessities for a lambing flock, a list too long and too boring to quote. John said three of the most important items were missing – plenty of Massey-Harris band, twice as many spare light bulbs as you think you will need and a good dog.

Massey-Harris band is Yorkshire for baling twine, and of course John was right. The first time I had to deliver a lamb unassisted (at an hour unpopular with vets and neighbours alike), the ewe refused to lie still. I doubled a length of twine, tied it round a front fetlock with a plough knot, drew the leg upward, passed the twine across the back of the ewe's neck, pulled it tight and attached the end to the other foreleg. Like it or not, and I suspect that she didn't, the ewe had to lie still. A piece of soft rope would have been better but none was to hand and the twine worked. Calves used to be trussed up like this when in transit in car boots.

Baling twine takes the place of wire, of rope, of staples and, occasionally, of braces. People say it's the badge of the lazy farmer. This to me is like insisting on tying sheaves while the combine stands idle. I was short of time and help. I improvised whenever possible. To this day, I use baling twine for every conceivable purpose. Most of the gates on the farm have wire mesh fastened along their bottoms to discourage young lambs from creeping underneath. John used to fasten the mesh with short pieces of wire twisted tight with pliers. It was hard on the hands and involved a lot of stooping. Yes, you may laugh at the little knots of blue and yellow twine which have replaced the wire fasteners, but the twine will last and can be tied on in minutes, so why not? I think they look rather pretty.

For some jobs, twine isn't strong enough, even doubled, but six thicknesses plaited make an almost unbreakable cord. These cords make blue and yellow leads for dogs, halters for rams and fasteners for gates.

My ewes were lucky. Still refusing the help of a dog, I kept them in a shed right under the windows when lambing time came round. I was expecting to have to rush out every couple of hours to make sure that all was well, but John reassured me. He told me to leave them alone from midnight until six a.m. unless one had started to lamb. He said I'd soon be an inefficient wreck if I didn't get enough sleep, and that the ewes wouldn't benefit from constantly being woken up any more than I would. He taught me to fill the hay racks after the midnight inspection, reckoning the ewes would lamb when they had fed and rested. Feeding at six, he said, was simply asking for a rush of lambs at three a.m.

In twenty-five years of lambing since then, I've followed his advice and hardly ever regretted it. City dwellers, who think of lambing time as one long stint in the maternity ward, may doubt this. Actually, the after-care and feeding of the ewes and their lambs takes up more time. Herding is the very essence of 'dog and stick' farming. I watched John, and wondered how to back down gracefully on the subject of a dog. Without one, you must walk right round the field, counting heads. Ewes leave their young lambs hidden when they go to feed, and finding them is time consuming. As soon as a dog appears in the field, even the familiar one they see every day, every ewe will call her lambs to her, so checking them takes only a few minutes.

Of course my thirty ewes were only a fraction of our sheep enterprise. John and the dogs were managing another 275 with much less fuss. Quite a number of new sheep farmers used to ask his advice, and I remember an earnest young man asking, 'What shall I do about my lambing average?'

'Do the same as everyone else,' said John cynically. 'Lie about it.'

The sheep tied in pretty well with our horsedealing. We didn't have much trade in the winter months, and there were no big fairs until Kilrush on March 25th. This was a day when John was content to sheep-sit, and I went to the fair on my own. Usually though, we went everywhere together. If one of us appeared alone, fellow dealers would ask, 'Where's the other one?'

I looked after the sheep when John was out hunting, and it was on one of these occasions that he fell and broke his leg, leaving me in charge of 350 ewes which had just started lambing.

This experience was unpleasant for John, who was sadly neglected. It did me a great deal of good, as it taught me just how much I could do. It also forced me to use that dog.

The dog in question was called Roy. Later, he served as a model for another Roy, a dog in a novel called *No Harp Like My Own*. Roy had had a hard life and was touchy and suspicious. Few people could win his confidence, let alone his affection. John succeeded, and so did I to a lesser extent. We were careful to keep him away from Diana, then a baby, but Roy was a different dog with her; patient and affectionate.

Once I had got used to working the sheep with Roy, I became bitten (to coin a phrase) with sheepdogs and sheepdog trials. John gave me a Border Collie bitch for myself, and I was soon breeding and selling puppies. The Crannagh kennel was registered around 1970.

All the dogs were different. There was Moyne, eager but slapdash, not too clever and an appalling mother; gentle, sensitive Tess, difficult, independent Meg and the old trial dog,

Billy. Billy disliked children, and was too temperamental to be top class, although he was runner up on 'One Man and his Dog', and won a good many trials. But after Roy, we didn't have a dog with as much personality until Dale arrived.

John, of course, had a way with dogs. This quality, difficult to define, has more to do with respect than with affection. Dogs obeyed John unhesitatingly, accepting him as master and friend in that order. He controlled them without force, knowing they would obey. John needed all his talents to cope with Dale. A pedigree Border Collie, he didn't look like one to anyone not familiar with the breed. His appearance hinted at gundog ancestry. He was tall and powerfully built, smooth coated, jet black with the distinctive white 'collar'. His domed skull and turned down ears resembled neither of his parents. Dale was a pack-leader without a pack to lead; a dog of active brain and great intelligence. He had boundless courage and, on occasions, a dreadful temper. This he inherited from his mother, a cattle bitch known as 'The Witless Savage'.

Mick, who owned the Savage (whose real name was Jess) also owned two of Dale's sisters. These he trained for sheepdog trials with mixed success, as both were handy with their teeth. They were known as 'Lamb Chops' and 'Frying Pan' to trial addicts. Mick remarked that they would fetch sheep – dead or alive. 'Sharpening up her knife and fork,' we used to say, as Frying Pan licked her chops, waiting for the flag to fall.

Dale fell into bad hands as a pup, suffering many beatings. They warped his nature but didn't break his spirit, as he learned to despise humans rather than fear them. John bought him for a song; a great overgrown puppy, eight months old, who could shift a herd of bullocks with ease. He had never been known to obey anyone, and would have been shot if John hadn't realised his potential.

John and Dale reached an understanding right away. John was boss, but Dale was allowed more latitude than his other dogs – his temperament required it. He walked beside John rather than at heel, asserting his equality, but he obeyed every

126

word, every tiniest signal, without question. At his best, I have never seen Dale's equal, on the trial field or off it.

For some reason, Yorkshireman John talked to Dale in the broadest of broad Yorkshire. I think it was a sign of affection, as Dale was his favourite. The other dogs were 'you', Dale was 'thoo'. 'Thoo daft sod,' John would say. 'Thoo big nowt. I'd shoot thee, but thoo isn't worth price of bullet – soft awd bugger.'

Dale interpreted this sort of thing correctly as a strange form of praise; he lashed his rope-like tail against his sides and grinned from ear to ear.

At that time, we had sixty suckler cows and two bulls. Dale marched them about like soldiers, never needing to use his formidable teeth. The cattle recognised his authority, just as Dale recognised John's.

When we went on holiday, Dale's previous owner persuaded John to let him look after him, promising that the dog would be exercised on a lead and chained up at night. But the temptation to work the reformed character was too strong. We heard afterwards that every flock of sheep within miles had been terrorised by the rogue dog.

Back home, Dale greeted John rapturously and they went off together to fetch sheep. The potential killer was particularly good with weak lambs, which he helped along by lifting their back ends gently with his nose and pushing them forward. No ewe ever dared to argue. About this time, a lamb fell into the river. Dale plunged in, swam after it, turned it and pushed it back, against the current, to a place where John could reach it with his crook. The lamb was half-drowned, but survived.

When John was out hunting, I would exercise Dale on a chain while he marched along beside me, his mind on other things. When I fed him, he wouldn't eat until I had gone. On the other hand, when John had to go away for a fortnight, Dale knew at once. He greeted me every day with grinning jaws and lashing tail, knowing there was nobody else around to feed and exercise him. I never dared to work him.

Naturally, I mated both my bitches with Dale, and expected them to breed champions; but few of his progeny turned out well. Probably because Dale himself was a sort of freak – a once-off model. His pups were too independent and prickly to take correction, while not having their sire's brilliance. Some were savage like their grandmother. An exception was a dog which we sold into Co Kildare, which saved a child's life. The boy was being attacked by some bullocks which, having just been treated with hormones, believed they were bulls. Young 'Glen' kept them off until help arrived, although they broke several of his ribs.

When Dale was six, in his prime, John and I went away for the day, leaving him in an outside kennel and run with the bitch, Moyne. I went to feed them when we got back. Moyne was waiting by her dish; Dale was lying in the night kennel with his nose on his paws. He was dead.

Dale had a flawed temperament – perhaps he had a flawed constitution too. I think he may have had a heart attack. We heard afterwards that strangers had been seen in the area, strangers who might have poisoned an aggressive dog. But greedy Moyne would have eaten the poison; Dale wouldn't have touched food if there were strangers about.

John didn't say much, although when I suggested a post mortem he snapped that it wouldn't bring Dale back. He went off to dig a grave in silence. Dale was such a big, heavy dog, weighing over fifty pounds, that I thought John would take his body away with the tractor, but no. He carried it in his arms. 'Thoo big, daft sod,' he said.

CHAPTER SIXTEEN

HAPPY DAYS

Life in the early 'seventies was wonderful. Everything was going our way, it seemed. The farm flourished, so did the dogs, and the horse trade was on the way up.

Mind you, I was lucky that I was not a widow. My wedding present to John had been a three year old horse, chosen more for his looks and his jumping ability than his temperament. He was a horse I couldn't have afforded if there hadn't been an 'if'. There were two ifs. One was a cold back, no matter how often he was ridden, the other was a slightly overshot jaw. Because of this, John called him 'Goose Neb' – I've forgotten his real name.

John and Goose Neb got on fine until one day when the horse caught his rider off guard – searching for a handkerchief,

I think. A moment later, a sky-high buck sent John crashing down on the cobbled yard. By the time he'd recovered from a fractured pelvis, I'd managed to sell the horse, which made an eventer for some reckless or suicidal rider.

Goose Neb wasn't the only sharp customer I wished on poor John. Before we were married, there was Clancy, illegitimate offspring of a thoroughbred yearling and a pony. He was as hard as nails and as slippery as an eel. Although I never fell off him, it was a near thing once or twice.

I remember taking him to a meet of the hounds which took place in Banbha Square in Nenagh, at a time when he should still have been in breaking tackle. When I tried to restrain his caperings, he ran backwards up the steps of the Provincial Bank, now the Garda Barracks, and bumped the swing doors open with his bottom. He then backed into the entrance hall, off the weathered stone and on to the polished Victorian tiles where he slithered wildly. As I wasn't on the friendliest of terms with my bank manager at the time, I thought it prudent to dismount and lead Clancy back down the steps. Somebody took rather a good picture of this, but I felt deeply humiliated. John got Clancy a few months later, and never had any trouble with him. Not so some of the people he tried to sell him to; the brains of a pony allied to the strength of a horse make a formidable combination.

Why is it that someone is invariably present with a camera when one is being publicly made a fool of? Why can't they be there when they might be appreciated? Another occasion which was immortalised in Banbha Square was the only time I can remember falling off a horse when it was actually standing still. This occurred at a holiday meet, in the middle of an interested crowd and under the nose of a photographer. The horse in question was called Timothy, a tall, narrow – very narrow – bay three year old. Riding him was rather like being astride a clothes line but, although dreadfully green, he was reasonably quiet. What I didn't know about him was that he had the trick of blowing himself out when his girths were being tightened. Only grass-fed ponies do this as a rule. I suppose I mounted when he was holding his breath, and forgot to check my girths. Anyway, in the middle of the crowded square, he let his breath go, gave a convulsive wriggle and somehow shot his saddle back almost to his loins. Both I and the saddle finished up underneath him, and it was lucky that he didn't seem disturbed by this, merely turning his head to peer at me in some surprise.

Writing about my horsedealing years in an earlier book, I think I gave the impression that I bought only in the fairs. This is misleading – about half my horses were bought off the land. Even today, buying off a farm is more expensive than waiting for a fair or sale. But it was, and is, the only thing to do if you need to secure a particular animal and daren't risk opposition.

In my early days, lack of a car obliged me to deal locally, at farms which were in reach of my bike. Some of the owners I met were great people to deal with, but sometimes I started a family feud when I wanted to buy a horse. One member would be keen to sell, another determined not to. Another would think – correctly – that if I was offering £50 and expecting profit, a private buyer would give more.

I remember a household consisting of an old brother and two old sisters. The brother, Denis, had told me he had a horse to sell, I went to the farm, and met him cycling down the laneway to meet me. 'You'll have to ask the sisters will they sell,' he said.

'You ask them,' I suggested.

'I will not,' Denis said. 'They're devils on wheels. You deal with them. Talk to Julia – she's the boss.'

Looking past him, I saw two elderly women standing, arms folded, outside the house. 'Which is Julia?' I asked nervously.

'Ah, you couldn't mistake Julia,' said her brother. 'You could wipe poison off her face.' With that, he grabbed his bike and pedalled off as fast as he could, probably to the nearest pub.

My nerve almost failed me – he was right about Julia – and I was glad when the horse turned out to be unsuitable. Years later, the same family was selling a daughter of this mare (which they had never managed to sell). I told John the above story and he laughed at me. '*I'll* deal with Julia,' he said confidently. I told him to go ahead, and refused to go along and see fair play. He returned routed, and the filly like its mother, stayed where it was.

A farmer with only one horse to sell would often overvalue it, certain that his goose was a swan. Especially deluded were two brothers, well up in their seventies, who were semi-retired. They had let most of their land and sold most of their stock. They retained two cows and a horse.

The horse, a quality bay gelding, was seven years old. The brothers had bred him and lovingly watched him grow into a nice sort of lightweight. He was not exceptional, not a show horse, but there would be no difficulty in selling such an animal. The problem was that in all his seven years he had never been haltered except, presumably, when he was castrated.

The hair-raising price asked left me speechless. The old men evidently thought they owned another Arkle. I explained that, even if I could have afforded him, their horse would be aware of his own strength. He would take a lot of breaking in. The old men listened pityingly and offered me a cup of tea.

Some weeks later, a well heeled customer from England came to my farm and bought a 'made' hunter. He showed me a list of several animals he had been told to go and see, and there was the two brothers' address at the top of the list. I reflected that a man who had been unwise enough to say that he had plenty of money probably had an employee capable of training a seven year old. I went with him to the farm, without warning or explanation.

When we arrived, we found the horse yoked to a 'Hunter hoe', scuffling turnips. True, one brother drove while the other led the horse, but he seemed quite placid. When my buyer wanted to see the horse ridden, I volunteered, but was quickly put in my place by one of the brothers. 'Don't mind her,' he said, 'she's in dread.' And he swarmed up on the horse's bare back.

They asked for, and got, the same outrageous price for him they had asked me, but with rather more justification this time. I'd like to be able to say that he was a success, but in England he turned out to be just about impossible. His new owner told me in a letter that he had an insensitive mouth and no respect for his rider.

'. . . there's no bucking, no rearing or plunging, just plain, straightforward bloody-mindedness. He's as strong as a bull and as obstinate as a mule . . .' A few days later, I met one of the brothers at a farm sale and he asked after the horse.

'He's in Leicestershire,' I said. 'They're finding him hard to manage.'

'Of course they are. He's lonesome – he was our pet. Write to the harmless man and tell him to give the horse five or six mangolds every night and plenty of work in chains. He'll be no trouble at the hunt if he's scuffled half an acre of swedes first.'

I passed on the advice, but it wasn't acknowledged and I suspect wasn't followed.

Buying off the land could be a protracted business; in fairs one had to be speedy – I avoid the word 'quick', because it's jargon for dishonest and might be misinterpreted. The horse fairs weren't anything like as rough and lawless as they have been represented, but at fairs, as in chain stores, buying bargains means acting decisively and fast. As for violence, much depends on what you mean by it. I once went to a big furniture auction and emerged bruised, battered and without any furniture because of the energy with which normally peaceful citizens, mostly female, had weighed in with hands, knees and sometimes feet in their determination to be to the fore. A small-town horse fair was a gentle affair by comparison. A modern sheep sale, where the buyers crowd round the pens (and I *mean* crowd), is rougher than any horse fair I have attended. And if that isn't rough enough for you, try a football match. The point is that if you are looking for violence, it is, and always has been, easily found.

There were a few people at the fairs who were well-known for their fragile tempers and awkward dispositions, and were avoided by dealers who didn't want trouble. I never had any problems with them. And there was one character who, although popular and easy-going, had a knack of finding himself in the middle of any rough-house that was going on. He never sought trouble but always found it – the exception that proves the rule. Possibly the company he kept had something to do with it.

This man, whom I will call Joe, frequented a pub in whose back room many differences had been sorted out, and had twice been attacked by a bad lot and had come off worst both times. Word went round that the attacker had started to carry a knife, so I will call him Mac. Joe's friends warned him about Mac's knife. They decided things had gone far enough and that it was time Mac cooled his heels in prison for a while.

Accordingly Joe, who was tall and stout, got his friends to wrap him from armpits to knees in a feather quilt, which they tied round him with string. A very large belted mackintosh completed the outfit. Joe planned to taunt Mac into drawing the knife, reckoning that the feathers would turn the blade. He would have all the witnesses he needed.

Mac arrived, spoiling for a fight, but he was bright as well as vicious and took in the situation at a glance. He punched Joe hard on the nose – not a matter for prison – and Joe, hampered by his quilt, crashed on to the floor. Mac then sat on him, drew the knife and used it to rip up the quilt, filling the room with musty feathers. He then left, and nobody tried to stop him.

I was not present on that occasion, but I did once see two elderly men fighting with sticks. It seemed to be an orderly affair, rather like a duel, and was judged by referees.

Most of the dealers who got involved with the seamy side of horse fairs were poor men. They were born dealers (like me), people who would rather sell at a loss and buy a worse one than not sell at all – and there is something to be said for this point of view. Some horses bought on spec are hard to place, even when they are good ones. Billy Bamlet, who bought so many of mine, used to ask if I had any 'dangling in the branches'. I often sold him a horse for cost or less when I had got tired of looking at it. Anything is better than swapping – the ultimate face-saver. The swapped-with may get rid of a misfit, but the instigator of the swap always comes off worst. When he realises this, he may swap again, losing every time. In the end, he will, as they say, be left with nothing but the halter.

Swapping in kind is a much better idea. I have always liked what is called a tinker's deal, when, instead of changing a bad horse for a worse one, you exchange him for a good cow or a suitable number of sheep. I have done both these things. I knew a man once who exchanged two cows for a litter of pigs and a piano, but he was drunk at the time. His wife, who had asked him to buy her a piano, was pleased, but thought he might have wrapped it up before loading it in the lorry with the pigs.

John went along with my passion for dealing, although he didn't share it. As long as I kept my hands off our breeding stock he was content to let me sell everything else. He did sometimes object to the people I dealt with, and he was usually right. One man had bought quite a number of horses from us, and I said at intervals, 'He's all right – you're just prejudiced.' He wasn't all right, as we discovered to our cost. An elderly woman summed him up nicely. 'I wouldn't lie against him for shelter,' she said, 'not if I had to go to Connacht for a bush.'

CHAPTER SEVENTEEN

SITTING IT OUT

The farming boom in the early 'seventies was, of course, a result of joining the Common Market; and like most rocketing rises, it was matched by a crash which put a lot of farmers out of business. We were lucky in having a diversity of projects. The cattle lost out while the horses and sheep saved us. There is nothing like a slump to teach caution – it concentrates the mind wonderfully. I was among the minority who had lived through the Economic War. Younger farmers seemed to think that the EEC would bring permanent riches for a minimum of effort and responded to the current advice to specialise. Too many eggs in one basket often meant the collapse of the whole basketful.

As we sat it out, we increased the lambing flock, because

wool was dear and so were the lightweight lambs needed by the new European market. We did without paid labour and took no risks. While the horse business was affected by the recession, our turnover was so fast that we were often buying and selling on the same day – the only way to deal on a falling market.

As for the sheep, when you manage a flock with no help except that of a dog, and with limited means, you have to aim for a high standard of quality in the lambs. When trade is bad, you can always sell good stock – though maybe at a bad price. If your stock is substandard you can go to market and stay there all day with no one, as they say, to ask you where you are going. I was often reminded of the maxims I had learned from my Yorkshire buyers. 'You can run to buy, but they make you stand to sell.' 'Any daft sod can stand on a street corner and buy dear horses – the day you buy is the day you sell.' Both these sayings are applicable to the daft sods who run to buy dear sheep, too.

I thought it would be a great idea to try giving the ewes fertility drugs, resulting in litters rather than pairs of lambs, all born within a few days. John pointed out that we would need expensive help and equipment to avoid heavy losses and, while science has given us litters of four and five lambs, it has not given us a ewe with more than two teats. There is also the question of luck – like having all your ewes timed to lamb on the worst day in living memory.

Sitting it out when sheep prices collapse isn't as traumatic as trying to feed a herd of cattle that nobody wants to buy. I have had to do it in the last few years and survived – just. I sold the older ewes and kept all my ewe lambs for breeding instead. This paid in the long run. I began to look round for other ways of staying solvent, among them writing, but more of that later. I bred more sheepdog pups. When obliged to sell the last of my lambs for half nothing, I instantly replaced them with females, also for half nothing. I am still sitting it out, awaiting better things. And of course I'm still dealing.

Livestock owners are divided into groups – those who buy and sell their own animals and those who employ a dealer or commission agent. Why should a farmer need a dealer to buy sheep from somebody else and sell them to him at a profit? Here's an example. When I once asked a newly fledged farmer whether he bought his sheep direct from the mart or from a dealer, he gave me a shocked look and said he did his marketing through *an entrepreneur*. There is a whole new language designed to make simple things complicated, and complicated things seem to the uncritical mind superior to simple ones. The difference between a dealer and *an entrepreneur*, when marketing livestock, is roughly the same as the difference between a commercial traveller and a sales representative.

A third group deals with suppliers who are linked with the factories where the animals end up. This method is popular, being reasonably foolproof. It also acts as a buffer between the cold reality of the factory and the tender hearted. To my mind, it turns the farmer himself into a middleman, unpaid at that, but other people don't seem to see it that way.

I have a rooted objection to allowing other people to spend my hard-earned money for me, and often wonder at the number of highly trained young farmers who allow their employees to choose and buy their stock. If the workman is such a good judge, why isn't he farming? The only reason I have been given is that an eye for stock is something you are born with or without, like an ear for music. I don't believe this. If it were true, a stock farmer without that 'eye' would be like a tone deaf person trying to keep a job in an orchestra. Ability to judge stock can be developed, and I advise would-be buyers to go to the markets and watch the people who buy and sell for a living. They would soon run out of money if they made mistakes.

Having been obliged to buy my own from the start, I made mistakes, but hadn't the means to make expensive ones. When illness prevented me from buying bullocks, I engaged a dealer and gave him commission, but made it clearly understood that, when the time came, I would expect him to sell the same animals – at a profit. He earned his commission.

Most of my buying experience has been gained with horses, when one major blunder could spell financial disaster. This has made me careful in buying all stock – no bad thing, I think. A dealer told me many years ago to ask myself three questions when buying a horse: Do I like the look of him? Is there improvement in him? Have I a market for him? 'If the answer to all three questions is "yes",' he said, 'you needn't ask yourself whether you can afford to pay for him; you can.' I think this advice holds good for any kind of livestock and I've followed it slavishly.

It's hard, when you are starting out, to screen the advice you are sure to get. 'Wise men don't need it: fools won't take it.' Some has to be followed, all is well-meant. It took me a while to resist advice to buy stock that I instinctively disliked. Instinct is often right, and the person who is paying is also going to have to look at the animals, so why not make it as pleasant as possible. The older I get, the more convinced I become that to do something well, you must enjoy it.

After the slump comes the recovery. A rising market is, of course, what every dealer needs. In Ireland, the cow was queen. The price of milk and the price of beef ruled everything else. When they rose, so in due course would the price of mutton, wool, and even riding horses. The first rise in prices which concerned me occurred when I was new to buying horses.

Everywhere there were rumours. 'The police are upping their prices . . . so are the Life Guards/Swiss Cavalry/Gunners . . .' Even the animals known as 'blood-testers' which were used by veterinary firms for developing vaccines, suddenly rose in price. I asked anyone who might know for information; none was forthcoming. This was part of the flip side of being a woman in a male-dominated profession. I never met with aggression or even scorn, but I was sometimes laughed at, fairly kindly. After a time I began to feel I had been accepted and there wasn't a problem – except the absence of loos at horse fairs.

The most galling thing I had to put up with was knowing that a lot of people assumed that a man must be financing me. I bought a half-spoiled filly in Limerick when I was about eighteen, and someone said to me, 'Whoever's paying for that one won't send you out for another.' I heard the same sort of comments when I was buying cattle. It has been suggested to me that people in England were less sexist, but I didn't find them so. For years, the man who bought police horses from me kept up the pretence with his customers that I was a man. I discovered this when I got a letter from a police representative starting, 'Dear Mr Smithwick . . .' I told this story to an elderly Irish dealer who said, 'I've nothing against women, but it's best not to tell them anything. What they don't know won't trouble them.' Sadly enough, there are still plenty who would agree with him – although not many who would admit it.

Here is a story which might or might not be true. It is about a strong farmer who kept a horse or two and also had a wife. I put them in that order deliberately. The man, who might have been called Jim, married lateish in life as a result of a September weekend in Lisdoonvarna.

Jim had been brought up to catch 'em young, treat 'em rough and tell 'em nothing, but so far had managed to avoid marriage. Mary, his bride, wasn't too young and she wasn't too bright. *She* had been brought up to be grateful if her husband didn't actually beat her, and she made the best of her bargain.

Jim, with about forty years of bachelorhood behind him, had no intention of altering his ways. He went to the pub five nights a week, went racing whenever there was a meeting within fifty miles and never missed a hurling match. At home, he was stingy, allowing Mary the bare minimum of cash to keep house. When she complained, he told her that times were hard. As it happened, he not only drew a hefty milk cheque

141

every month, but was drinking and betting his way through a sizeable fortune which his uncle had left him.

Mary, poor harmless woman, was sorry for Jim and never asked for money for herself, but she heard talk . . . She started asking how much the bullocks had fetched at the mart, how the barley had done, how much the foal had fetched. Jim now found it expedient to lie. He hastily banked a cheque for £5,000 and said, 'The cattle only made a few hundreds – the trade is gone to hell.' As for the fine colt foal which he'd sold for a thousand, Jim said, 'He paid for his stud fee and a little shake along of it. It doesn't do to grumble.' This was when £1,000 was a crazy price for a half-bred foal. Jim's horses always paid well, but he sold only one or two a year. His best was a yearling, which he expected would fetch £2,000.

As he set off for Galway races, Jim said to Mary, 'I advertised the yearling in *Farmers' Journal* this week. If anyone calls to see him, tell them I'll be here on Sunday.'

'How much are you expecting to get for him?' Mary asked.

'He might make two,' said Jim, who was in a hurry and off his guard for once. 'I'd be delighted if he did.'

'Only two?' Mary asked doubtfully. 'I didn't think they were as cheap as that.' But Jim thought she was being sarcastic and didn't bother to answer.

At Galway races it never stopped raining and all the favourites lost. Jack drowned his sorrows in every pub on his way home, and arrived in the small hours in a bad temper. He was surprised to find Mary waiting up for him; sitting in the kitchen with a broad smile on her face. 'I sold the colt for you,' she said. 'The man said he couldn't wait for you and I was afraid he mightn't come back, so I collected the cash.' She counted out ten £20 notes on the table.

'Where's the rest?' Jim asked.

'It's all there – £200 – what you said you'd be glad to take. He was a grand man,' she went on, 'I wish you'd been here to meet him. What's this he said his name was? I forget. I didn't bother too much when he was paying cash. Should I have? He wouldn't even take a fiver back for luck. He loaded up the colt and away he went.'

Jim broke in with an angry roar. 'I meant thousands, not hundreds,' he bellowed. 'Two grand, woman! Don't you know anything about the price of a horse?' he screamed, tearing his hair.

'Only what you've told me yourself,' Mary said, staring at him in amazement. 'You said you only got four hundred for the brown mare.'

Jim's yearling had disappeared as completely and permanently as Shergar. All the neighbours had been at the races or watching the Galway Plate on television. Nobody had seen a medium sized man driving a medium sized car which might have been cream or grey, and whose make and number Mary couldn't remember. Neither could she recall anything about the trailer. It might have been grey, she thought. And no, the man hadn't asked for any papers for the colt.

Jim was the laughing stock of the countryside when the story got out. 'You made a right fool of me,' he said to Mary. 'I'll have to go away until it's all forgotten.'

'That's a great notion,' said Mary. 'Will we go to Lisdoon-varna for a fortnight?'

CHAPTER EIGHTEEN

A LATE VOCATION

When beef prices crashed in 1974, recession in Britain was hitting the horse trade and I had an unpleasant interlude in hospital. We redoubled our efforts to make a living in half a dozen ways at once. At the same time, my mother's continuing illness (she died in 1979) kept me housebound for a lot of the time.

While trying to do most of my horse business on the phone, I rediscovered a minor artistic talent and put it to use painting souvenirs. I did quite well for a time, although nobody was amused by beer mugs with 'Guinness is bad for you' painted on them. Then I began to get orders for a couple of hundred handpainted mugs at a go, and a mildly profitable hobby became a demanding chore. Soon I was suffering from eyestrain and terminal boredom. Machine knitting and weaving were little better. The only thing which paid while also giving me pleasure was the breeding of Border Collies. We were putting together a kennel of useful dogs which combined good temperaments with ability, and puppies sold like hot cakes. John and I went to sheepdog trials most Sundays and spent our time deep in conversation with kindred spirits.

There are two approaches to selling puppies. One is the 'I don't care as long as they pay' school, reminiscent of the dealer who said 'If a customer comes back for a second horse, I know I didn't charge enough for the first one'. The other viewpoint is that nobody else in Ireland could possibly appreciate and look after your puppy. It is sure to be ill-treated, starved, neglected – how can you be such a monster as to part with it? I wept when I sold my first eight week old puppy. The last of the litter of seven was sold with relief; the puppies were now hungry young dogs, demanding quantities of food, exercise and attention. Like most breeders of pedigree stock, I learned to part with my favourites philosophically. Soon, I had so much demand for puppies that I could discourage anybody who seemed unlikely to appreciate one.

One thing which became tedious was answering all the questions which each buyer in turn asked. The same questions over and over again: What does he eat? When does he get his jabs? When do we start to train him? So I wrote out an eight hundred word guide, entitled, *Looking after your sheepdog puppy*. This I proposed to have photocopied, so that I could hand one over with every pup. I can remember how carefully I penned the two pages of foolscap in my best script, with plenty of red underlining, and how pleased I was with the effect. Like other watersheds in my life, it went unrecognised at the time. I was fifty-one years old and not planning on a new career. John vetted my work and said, 'Why don't you offer it to *Farmers' Journal* as an article?'

Fools rush in. I went straight to the telephone, asked for the editor and gave him an outline of what I'd written. When I put the phone down ten minutes later, I'd been commissioned to write a series of six articles entitled *The Farm Dog* at £25 apiece. This stretched to ten articles and £30, and almost before I knew it, I was a freelance journalist, writing for the main Irish farming magazines on a variety of dog- and sheep-related subjects. A year later, I had my first article accepted by *The Irish Field*, extending my repertoire to horses.

I had been brought up on tales of my literary forbears. Edith Somerville was my grandmother's first cousin and they used to share their holidays as girls. I have a sketchbook of Granny's with painstaking drawings of architecture, while the blank pages facing them are covered with Edith's caricatures and cartoons. Then there was Henry Seton Merriman (a nom de plume), a wildly fashionable novelist of the early part of the century, now hopelessly dated. Other relatives were the naturalist and writer Ernest Thomson Seton, father of Anya Seton. More recently, my aunt, Evelyn Brodhurst-Hill, had written two successful books of memoirs and had had many political articles published in *The Spectator*. I found these facts daunting rather than encouraging. When I said as a girl that I'd like to be a writer, all these people were held up as examples of what I could do if I tried. I didn't try.

I slunk into writing through the back door. After the first batch of articles, I tried to brighten up a (then) rather solemn magazine called *Working Sheepdog News* with a story called *Shep at the Sheepdog Trial*. Greatly to my surprise, this resulted in a spate of letters demanding 'more about Irish Shep'. This work was unpaid at the time, but it was great fun, and I soon wrote about twenty episodes. What started as separate funny pieces gradually became a narrative. I discovered I was writing a book.

Meanwhile, I'd got the original twelve sheepdog articles printed and bound by a firm which deals mainly with posters and dance tickets. To my utter astonishment, I sold a thousand copies and had to print more. It sold 2,000 copies all told.

Author Charles Chenevix Trench, a friend of ours, then did me the good turn of a lifetime by sending my 'Shep' stories to his agent, David Fletcher, in Edinburgh. It is well known that you can't get an agent unless you are published, and you can't get published unless you have an agent. David sent the manuscript, entitled *One Dog and his Man* to eight publishers, and they all returned it except for two firms which lost it between them, each blaming the other. The ninth publisher, approached without much hope, was the Blackstaff Press, who accepted it. It appeared in 1984 and had the best notices I've ever received. Phrases like 'a little gem', 'a small masterpiece', and many more littered the reviews. I was asked for, and wrote, a sequel. *Pelham Books* commissioned a large handsome hardback about Border Collies, stuffed with photographs. I was in seventh heaven. A writer. Good God – me! Well, there it was, and now I could write a novel and it would be published and I would be fêted and fussed over . . . rich . . . famous . . .

Long before my feet had returned to the ground, I had a letter from Collins, commissioning a novel. This threw me into a tremendous tizzy but obviously it wasn't an offer I could refuse. John had given me a course with The Writing School as a present, and I'd found it helpful in writing articles, although I don't think I learned much about novel-writing from it. However, my tutor had constantly encouraged me to try a novel; so, faced with the task of writing a 90,000 word book (my 'Shep' books were only a third of that length) I wrote to him for help. I received the support I needed – as much confidence boosting as actual tuition – and set to work. The book, *Corporal Jack* was – you've guessed it – about a dog.

The whole of the writing of this book was overshadowed by John's illness and death. Sometimes I wonder how it was possible to write at all; more often I wonder how I could have got through those months without something demanding to do which had to be completed on time. It isn't a time I want to dwell on. I finished the book, physically and emotionally exhausted, and although Collins published it, and it did well, I can never think about it without remembering the circumstances of its writing.

The dog, Jack, was central to the plot, but I resisted writing a straight 'doggy' novel. Especially so as the book was set in the mud and blood of the First World War, and I felt that a dog hero somehow belittled the human characters. I managed to make the dog into the lynchpin which held the story together while retaining separate plots concerning a large cast of characters, and people liked the result.

I was then ready to embark on something totally different, but my idea for a new novel was rejected because there wasn't a dog in it. If Collins was to commission it I would have, they told me, to do a rethink. I rethought, and the resulting book, *No Harp Like My Own*, became my biggest financial success to date. I had had to contrive somewhat in order to introduce a dog, and to make the dog important without losing my basic idea, but I thought I had done so without loss of integrity.

Apparently not. Around then, I went to a launch where I met a poet who told me that my work wouldn't be worth reading if I bent in any way to the will of publishers and editors. I told him what I'd done, murmuring that those who were paying me presumably knew what they were doing. The poet shuddered. 'I suppose you realise you've prostituted your soul,' he said. Ah, well.

After this, I tried even harder to get away from the 'doggy' label. I offered various ideas around but always got the same reaction. 'Where's the dog?'

Well, I have stood fast in my refusal to write about dogs all the time, and have got by. Every branch of writing has its own pitfalls, and those which await the animal writer are deeper and nastier than most. I have learned to be wary of the sort of blurb which begins, 'This is the story of a man, a woman and a dog,' or 'This heart-warming tale will delight animal lovers everywhere.'

149

Reviewers seem to feel it their duty to belittle novels which feature animals, with patronising allusions to Lassie and Black Beauty. And without reviews, the modern writer withers and dies. Sometimes people say that writing about animals is easier than writing about humans. It may be, but it carries the temptation to indulge in sentimentality. Funny – sentimentality is foreign to animals and small children, yet stories about both are often saccharine-sweet.

It is a fact that some of us are utterly devoted to our pets. I believe it's the knowledge that their lives are short which makes us love them so much – that and our own need for selfless devotion. This is all very well, but incredibly hard to express in fiction. There is only a hairline between genuine pathos and mawkish sentimentality.

I avoided writing another doggy book the next time, but only by substituting horses. André Deutsch published my first book of memoirs, *Breakfast the Night Before*, and were also the first to accept from me a novel with no animal interest. Children's books followed. But my illusions about making a lot of money by writing have faded. To succeed financially, I really believe you must find a niche and firmly stay in it, resisting all temptations to experiment. I still farm for my bread and butter – my books have provided the jam.

And now recession has brought a jam shortage, just when hard times in agriculture have cut down the bread and butter ration. So, up to a point, it's back to the hard slog. And this has been a hard book to write, because I have tried to deal with the different lives I've led; as horsedealer, farmer, dog-breeder and writer. If I have included little about my husband and daughter, it is only because that would have been John's wish, and is Diana's.

I am a firm believer in luck and an unsinkable optimist, which helps in times like these. And writing is something you can do as long as you can stay alive and retain your sanity. I love it (except when deadlines threaten) and I love the spin-offs that come with it. Through writing, I have got to know some delightful people I would otherwise never have met, and my horizons have been widened, which was certainly no harm. I have begun to live again after a bad patch.

As for the rest, the dogs are a continuing interest, and enable me to look after my sheep, for you need more than to be alive and reasonably sane if you are to farm. I also have willing helpers in my daughter and son-in-law.

The things which keep me going are new interests, new doors opening on the future – and I have just been given a very welcome one. I have become acquainted with a young person without whose help this book would have been finished weeks ago: my grandson, Jack, born on Christmas Day in the morning.

Marjorie Quarton, March 25, 1992